GREAT GOSPEL HYMNS

Compiled by

Mosie Lister • Tom Fettke • Ken Bible • Marty Parks
John Mathias • George Baldwin

Edited by
Marty Parks and Ken Bible

Lillenas® PUBLISHING COMPANY
KANSAS CITY, MO 64141

He Touched Me

William J. Gaither William J. Gaither

2 Boundless Love

Diane Wilkinson

Diane Wilkinson
Arranged by Marty Parks

I'll Fly Away

Albert E. Brumley

Albert E. Brumley

4 Goodby, World, Goodby

Mosie Lister | Mosie Lister

REFRAIN
Now don't you weep for me when I'm gone, 'Cause I won't have to leave here a - lone;
And when I hear that last trum - pet sound, My feet won't stay on the ground.
Gon - na rise with a shout, gon - na fly;
Gon - na ride with my Lord through the sky.
Heav - en is near, and I can't stay here, Good - by, world, good - by.

5 He Set Me Free

Albert E. Brumley — Albert E. Brumley

I've Been Changed

6

Mosie Lister — Mosie Lister

7 WELCOME, HOLY SPIRIT

A Hymn Sequence

Holy Spirit, Thou Art Welcome
The Comforter Has Come
He is Here

8 Holy Spirit, Thou Art Welcome

Dottie Rambo and David Huntsinger | Dottie Rambo and David Huntsinger

Optional segue to "The Comforter Has Come"
No transition is needed.

9 The Comforter Has Come

Frank Bottome | William J. Kirkpatrick

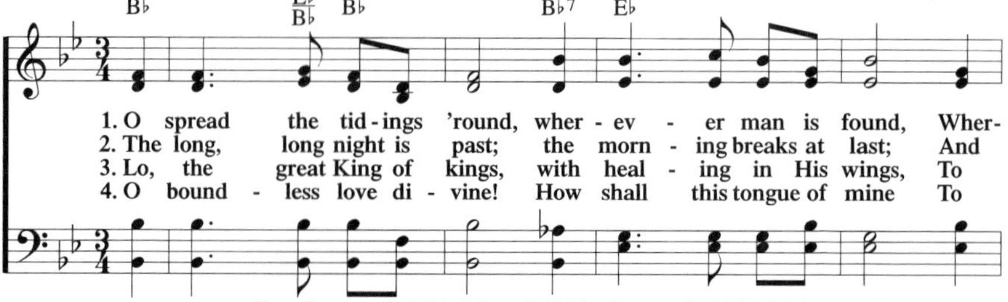

ev - er hu-man hearts and hu - man woes a - bound. Let ev - ery Chris-tian
hushed the dread-ful wail and fu - ry of the blast, As o'er the gold-en
ev - ery cap-tive soul a full de-liv-'rance brings; And thro' the va-cant
won - d'ring mor-tals tell the match - less grace di - vine– That I, a child of
tongue pro-claim the joy-ful sound: The Com - fort - er has come!
hills the day ad-vanc-es fast! The Com - fort - er has come!
cells the song of tri-umph rings: The Com - fort - er has come!
hell, should in His im-age shine! The Com - fort - er has come!
REFRAIN
The Com - fort - er has come! The Com - fort - er has come! The Ho - ly
Ghost from heav'n, the Fa - ther's prom-ise giv'n! O spread the tid-ings
'round, wher - ev - er man is found: The Com - fort - er has come!

Optional Transition to "He Is Here"

10 He Is Here

Kirk Talley

Kirk Talley
Arranged by Marty Parks

End of Hymn Sequence "WELCOME, HOLY SPIRIT"

Jesus Is Lord of All

Gloria Gaither and William J. Gaither | William J. Gaither

12 I Will Sing of My Redeemer

Philip P. Bliss

James McGranahan

Magnify Him

13

Randy Vader and Kirk Talley

Kirk Talley
Arranged by Marty Parks

14 How Great Thou Art

Stuart K. Hine Stuart K. Hine

Great is the Lord and most worthy of praise;
his greatness no one can fathom.
One generation will commend your works to another;
they will tell of your mighty acts.
They will speak of the glorious splendor of your majesty,
and I will mediate on your wonderful works.
They will celebrate your abundant goodness
and joyfully sing of your righteousness.

Psalm 145:3-5, 7

15 Because He Lives

Gloria Gaither and William J. Gaither — William J. Gaither

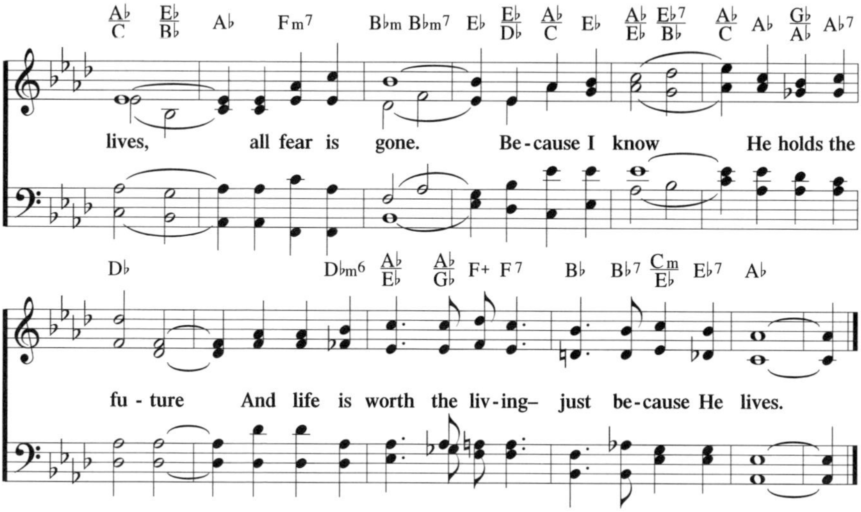

Hallelujah, Praise the Lamb **16**

P. T., D. T. and G. M.

Pam Thum, Dawn Thomas
and Gary McSpadden

17 I Bowed on My Knees and Cried, "Holy"

Anonymous E. M. Dudley Cantwell

B♭ F7/C Cm7 F7 B♭ B♭7
1. I dreamed of a cit - y called Glo - ry, so
2. When I en - tered the gates to the cit - y, my
3. I thought, when I saw my Re - deem - er, "Oh,
E♭ F/E♭ E♭ B♭ B♭/D F F2 F
bright and so fair. When I en - tered the
friends knew me well. They showed me
glo - ry to God!" I fell right
F7 E♭/F F7 B♭ B♭/A Gm7 Gm/C Gm7/C C7 C6 C7
gate I cried, "Ho - ly!" the an - gels all met me
all through heav - en; the scenes were to num - 'rous to
down be - fore Him, sing-ing praise to the name of the
F7sus F7 B♭ F7 E♭/G F7/A B♭
there. They showed me from man - sion to man - sion,
tell. I saw A - bra - ham, I - saac and Ja - cob,
Lord. I bowed down and wor - shipped Je - ho - vah,

B♭7/D E♭ E♭/G F F9 B♭
and, oh, the sights I saw. I
Mark, Luke and Tim - o - thy; But I
my Friend of Cal - va - ry. I
E♭ E♭M7 E°7 A/E E°7 B♭/F Gm B♭/F
said, "I want to see Je - sus, the One who
said, "I want to see Je - sus, the One who
want - ed to give praise to Je - sus for sav - ing a
F7 E♭/F F7 B♭
died for all."
died for me."
sin - ner like me.
REFRAIN
B♭7/D E♭ F/E♭ E♭
Then I bowed on my knees and cried,
B♭ F7/C F7 E♭/B♭ B♭ B♭7/D E♭
"Ho - ly, ho - ly, ho - ly." I clapped my
F/E♭ E♭ B♭ B♭/F B♭/D F7/C Cm7 F7 B♭
hands and sang, "Glo - ry, glo - ry to the Son of God."

18 Victory in Jesus

Eugene M. Bartlett Eugene M. Bartlett

1. I heard an old, old sto - ry, how a Sav - ior came from glo - ry,
2. I heard a - bout His heal - ing, of His cleans - ing pow'r re - veal - ing,
3. I heard a - bout a man - sion He has built for me in glo - ry,
How He gave His life on Cal - va - ry to save a wretch like me.
How He made the lame to walk a - gain and caused the blind to see.
And I heard a - bout the streets of gold be - yond the crys - tal sea,
I heard a - bout His groan - ing, of His pre - cious blood's a - ton - ing,
And then I cried, "Dear Je - sus, come and heal my bro - ken spir - it,"
A - bout the an - gels sing - ing, and the old re - demp - tion sto - ry;
Then I re - pent - ed of my sins and won the vic - to - ry.
And some - how Je - sus came and brought to me the vic - to - ry.
And some sweet day I'll sing up there the song of vic - to - ry.
REFRAIN
O vic - to - ry in Je - sus, my Sav - ior for - ev - er! He sought me and

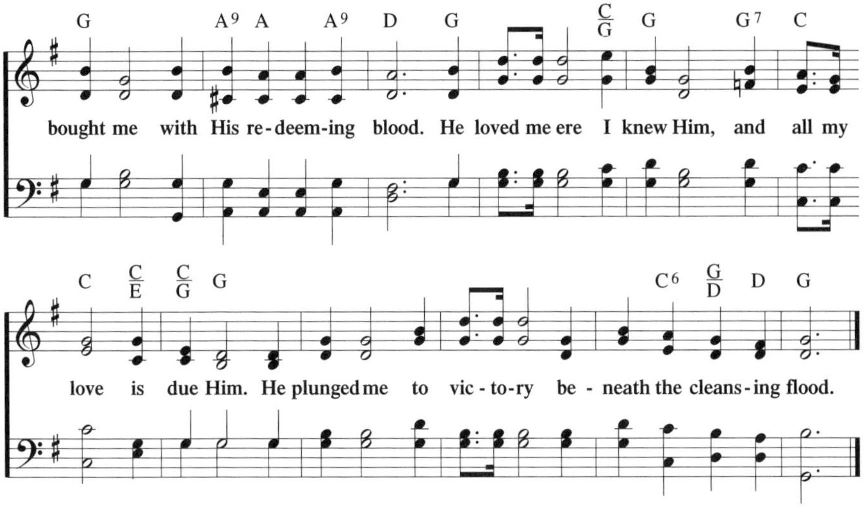
G A9 A A9 D G C/G G G7 C
bought me with His re-deem-ing blood. He loved me ere I knew Him, and all my
C C/E C/G G C6 G/D D G
love is due Him. He plunged me to vic-to-ry be - neath the cleans-ing flood.

Then Peter stood up with the Eleven, raised his voice, and addressed the crowd: "Fellow Jews and all of you who live in Jerusalem, let me explain this to you; listen carefully to what I say.

"Jesus of Nazareth was a man accredited by God to you by miracles, wonders and signs, which God did among you through him, as you yourselves know. This man was handed over by God's set purpose and foreknowledge; and you, with the help of wicked men, put him to death by nailing him to the cross. But God raised him from the dead, freeing him from the agony of death, because it was impossible for death to keep its hold on him.

"God has raised this Jesus to life, and we are all witnesses of the fact. Exalted to the right hand of God, he has received from the Father the promised Holy Spirit and has poured out what you now see and hear.

"God has made this Jesus, whom you crucified, both Lord and Christ.

"Repent and be baptized, every one of you, in the name of Jesus Christ for the forgiveness of your sins. And you will receive the gift of the Holy Spirit. The pomise is for you and your children and for all who are far off–for all whom the Lord our God will call."

Acts 2:14, 22-24, 32-33, 36, 38-39

19 Love Through Me

Mosie Lister

Mosie Lister

1. Love thro' me, love thro' me; O Lord, love thro' me.
2. Weep thro' me, weep thro' me; O Lord, weep thro' me.
3. Speak thro' me, speak thro' me; O Lord, speak thro' me.

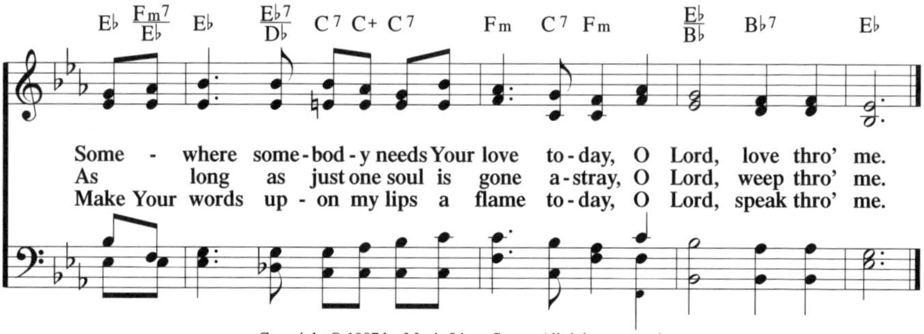
Some - where some-bod-y needs Your love to-day, O Lord, love thro' me.
As long as just one soul is gone a-stray, O Lord, weep thro' me.
Make Your words up - on my lips a flame to-day, O Lord, speak thro' me.

20 ABUNDANT GRACE

A Hymn Sequence

He Giveth More Grace
His Grace Is Sufficient for Me

21 He Giveth More Grace

Annie Johnson Flint

Hubert Mitchell

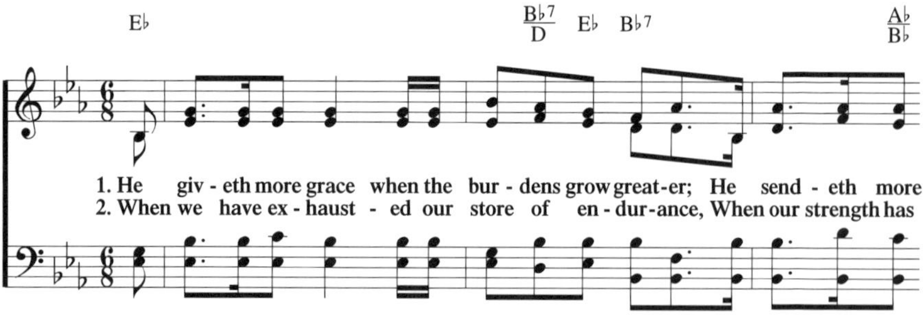
1. He giv - eth more grace when the bur - dens grow great-er; He send - eth more
2. When we have ex - haust - ed our store of en - dur-ance, When our strength has

B♭7 B♭9 B♭7/D E♭ E♭/G B♭7/F E♭7
strength when the labors increase. To added affliction He
failed ere the day is half done. When we reach the end of our
A♭ A♭7 E♭6 E♭ E♭7/G A♭6 E♭/B♭ B♭7 E♭
addeth His mercy; To multiplied trials, His multiplied peace.
hoarded resources, Our Father's full giving is only begun.
REFRAIN
E♭ B♭ B♭/A♭ E♭/G B♭7/F B♭ E♭ B♭7/F E♭/G E♭ A♭
His love has no limit; His grace has no measure. His pow'r has no
A♭ B♭/A♭ A♭ E♭ F7/C B♭sus B♭7 B♭7/F E♭
boundary known unto man. For out of His infinite
A♭/E♭ B♭/A♭ A♭ A♭/E♭ E♭ C7 G°7 Fm/A♭ E♭/B♭ B♭7 E♭
riches in Jesus, He giveth, and giveth, and giveth again!

Optional transition to "His Grace Is Sufficient for Me"

22 His Grace Is Sufficient for Me

Mosie Lister Mosie Lister

1. Man - y times I'm tried and test-ed as I trav - el day by day;
2. When the temp - ter bring con - fu - sion and I don't know what to do,
Oft I meet with pain and sor-row, and there's trou - ble in the way.
On my knees I turn to Je - sus, for I know He'll see me through.
But I have the sweet as - sur-rance that my soul the Lord will lead,
Then de - spair is changed to vic - t'ry, ev - ery doubt just melts a - way,

D♭ A♭/E♭ F7 B♭ B♭7 Cm/E♭ E♭7 A♭ D♭/A♭ A♭
And in Him there is strength for ev - ery need.
And in Him there is hope for ev - ery day.
REFRAIN
A♭ E♭7 D♭ A♭ D♭/A♭ A♭
O His grace is suf - fi - cient for me,
for me,
A♭ E♭7 D♭ A♭ D♭/A♭ A♭
And His love is a - bun - dant and free;
so free;
A♭ C C7 Fm
And what joy fills my soul just to know, just to know
D♭ A♭/E♭ F7 B♭ B♭7 E♭7 D♭/E♭ A♭ D♭/A♭ A♭
That His grace is suf - fi - cient for me!
for me!

End of Hymn Sequence "ABUNDANT GRACE"

23 Then I Met the Master

Mosie Lister | Mosie Lister

1. Like a babe when it cries for its moth-er, Like a child, I was help-less, a-lone. Then I met the Mas-ter; Now I am one of His own.
2. Like a blind man who walks in the dark-ness, I had longed, I had searched for the light. Then I met the Mas-ter; Now I walk no more in the night.
REFRAIN
For all things were changed when He found me; A new day broke thro' all a-round me; For I met the Mas-ter, Now I be-long to Him
Song ending
Optional ending after final refrain
long to Him. I met the Mas-ter; Now I be-long to Him.

There's Something About That Name 24

William J. Gaither and Gloria Gaither

William J. Gaither

E♭ E♭M7 B♭m E♭7 A♭ A♭m6
Je - sus, Je - sus, Je - sus! There's just some - thing a - bout that
E♭ A♭/B♭ E♭ Gm B♭m6/D♭ B♭m7/D♭ C7 F7sus
name! Mas - ter, Sav - ior, Je - sus! Like the fra - grance
F9 Dm/F F7 B♭9sus B♭7 E♭ E♭M7 B♭m E♭7
af - ter the rain. Je - sus, Je - sus, Je - sus! Let all
A♭ Fm/A♭ A♭7 Gsus G7 C G7/D C7/E C7
heav - en and earth pro - claim: Kings and king - doms will
F7sus F7 Fm7 Fm2/C Gm/B♭ B♭13 E♭
all pass a - way, But there's some - thing a - bout that name!

25 O For a Thousand Tongues

David Binion

David Binion
Arranged by Marty Parks

G C/G G G9/D F/C C Am
1. Glo - ry to the Lamb Whose throne for-
2. We crown You with sing-ing, Our lips shall
E7 Am2 Am D7 D#°7
ev - er reigns; God in the
ut - er Your praise; In hum - ble ad - o-
Esus Em Bm Em Esus Em Am Am7 D7
high-est, Worth-y to mer - it our praise.
ra - tion, In end - less re - frain.
REFRAIN
Am Bm/A C/D D7 C/G G Am Bm/A
O for a thou - sand tongues to sing prais - es
C/D D7 G2 G C/G G F/G G7
un - to Thee; O for a thou - sand

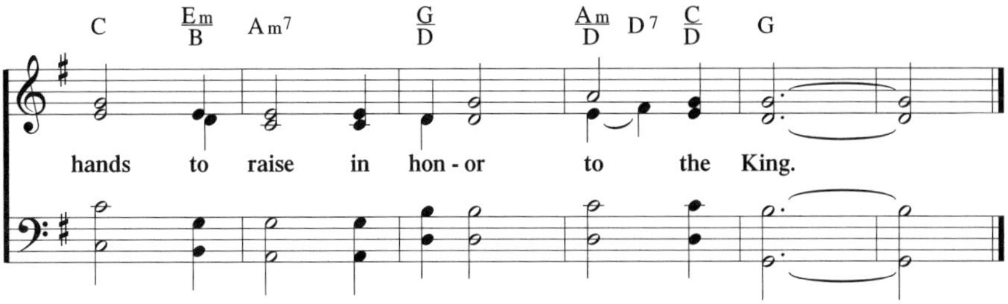
C Em/B Am7 G/D Am/D D7 C/D G
hands to raise in hon - or to the King.

Holy Ground

26

Geron Davis

Geron Davis
Arranged by Marty Parks

F C13 F C7sus/G C7/G F2/A F/A B♭ F/A C7/G F
We are stand - ing on ho - ly ground;
ground, ho - ly ground;
B♭ A7♭5 D7 D+ D7 G G/B B♭m6
And I know that there are an-gels all a - round.
B♭m6 B♭m(M7) F/A C7sus/G C7/G F2 F B♭ F/A C7/G F
Let us praise Je - sus now,
praise, Let us praise now, Je - sus now,
B♭ F/A B♭ F/C Am/C C7 B♭/C Fsus C7sus F
We are stand - ing in His pres-ence on ho - ly ground.
ground, ho - ly ground.

27 GLORY TO JESUS!

A Hymn Sequence

Glory to His Name
Blessed Be the Name

28 Glory to His Name

Elisha A. Hoffman — John H. Stockton

G G/B C C/E G
1. Down at the cross where my Sav - ior died, Down where for
2. I am so won - drous - ly saved from sin; Je - sus so
3. O pre-cious foun - tain that saves from sin! I am so
4. Come to this foun - tain so rich and sweet; Cast thy poor
G D G G/B C C/E G
cleans-ing from sin I cried, There to my heart was the blood ap - plied.
sweet - ly a - bides with - in. There at the cross where He took me in–
glad that I en - tered in! There Je - sus saves me and keeps me clean.
soul at the Sav - ior's feet; Plunge in to - day and be made com - plete.
G/D D7 G REFRAIN C G Gsus G G/B
Glo - ry to His name! Glo - ry to His name, Glo - ry to His
D G/D D G G/B C C/E G G/D D7 G
name! There to my heart was the blood ap - plied; Glo - ry to His name!

Optional transition to "Blessed Be the Name"

Blessed Be the Name

Charles Wesley;
refrain, Ralph E. Hudson

Anonymous

1. O for a thou - sand tongues to sing– Bless - ed be the name of the Lord!
2. Je - sus, the name that charms our fears– Bless - ed be the name of the Lord!
3. He breaks the pow'r of can - celled sin– Bless - ed be the name of the Lord!
The glo - ries of my God and King– Bless - ed be the name of the Lord!
'Tis mu - sic in the sin - ner's ears– Bless - ed be the name of the Lord!
His blood can make the foul - est clean– Bless - ed be the name of the Lord!
REFRAIN
Bless-ed be the name, bless-ed be the name; Bless-ed be the name of the Lord!
Bless-ed be the name, bless-ed be the name; Bless - ed be the name of the Lord!

End of Hymn Sequence "GLORY TO JESUS!"

30 I'm Bound for That City

Albert, Bill, Tom, Bob and James Brumley

Albert, Bill, Tom, Bob and James Brumley

1. There's a city of light where there cometh no night, For the sun never sets in the sky; In the Bible we're told that the streets are pure gold, And a cool, gentle river runs by.
2. Little children will play, and our hearts will be gay, As we stroll thro' that city of gold; No more dying up there, no more sorrow to bear, And nobody will be feeble and old.

REFRAIN
I'm bound for that cit - y, God's ho - ly, white
cit - y, O yes, I am; I'll nev - er turn back to this
world an - y - more; No mat - ter how rough may be the
more, an - y - more;
way. No mat - ter how oft I stop to pray, I'm bound for that
cit - y on that ev - er - green shore.
shore, ev - er - green shore.

31 This World Is Not My Home

Anonymous

Anonymous
Arranged by Marty Parks

1. This world is not my home, I'm just a - pass - ing thro'; My treas-ures are laid up some-where be-yond the blue. The an-gels beck-on me from heav - en's o - pen door, And I can't feel at home in this world an-y - more.
2. They're all ex-pect-ing me, and that's one thing I know, My Sav - ior par-doned me, and now I on-ward go; I know He'll take me thro' though I am weak and poor, And I can't feel at home in this world an-y - more.
3. Just up on glo - ry - land we'll live e - ter - nal - ly, The saints on ev - ery hand are shout-ing vic - to - ry. Their songs of sweet-est praise drift back from heav-en's shore, And I can't feel at home in this world an-y - more.
REFRAIN
O Lord, You know I have no friend like you; If heav - en's not my home, then, Lord, what will I do? The an - gels beck - on me from

heav-en's o-pen door, And I can't feel at home in this world an-y-more.

Just a Closer Walk with Thee

Anonymous

Anonymous

1. I am weak but Thou art strong; Je - sus, keep me from all wrong;
2. Thro' this world of toil and snares, If I fal-ter, Lord, who cares?
3. When my fee-ble life is o'er, Time for me will be no more;
I'll be sat-is-fied as long As I walk, let me walk, close to Thee.
Who with me my bur-den shares? None but Thee, dear Lord, none but Thee.
Guide me gent-ly, safe-ly o'er To Thy king-dom shore, to Thy shore.
REFRAIN
Just a clos-er walk with Thee– Grant it, Je-sus, is my plea,
Dai - ly walk-ing close to Thee– Let it be, dear Lord, let it be.

33 I Believe In a Hill Called Mount Calvary

William J. and Gloria Gaither,
Dale Oldham

William J. Gaither

G6 G7 C Csus C F G/F F C F/C C
1. There are things, as we trav - el this earth's shift - ing sands,
2. I be - lieve that the Christ who was slain on the cross
3. I be - lieve that his life with its great mys - ter - ies
C G7 F/G G6 G7 G6 G7 C2 C CM7 C
That tran - scend all the rea - son of man.
Has the pow - er to change lives to - day.
Sure - ly some - day will come to an end.
C7/G F Fm C F/C C
But the things that mat - ter the most in the world,
For He changed me com - plete-ly– a new life is mine.
But faith will con - quer the dark - ness and death,
C G7 F/G G7 F/G G7 C
They can nev - er be held in our hand.
That is why by the cross I will stay.
And will lead me at last to my friend.

REFRAIN
I be - lieve in a hill called Mount Cal - v'ry;
I be - lieve, what - ev - er the cost.
And when time has sur - ren - dered and earth is no more,
I'll still cling to the old rug - ged cross.
old rug - ged cross.

Jews demand miraculous signs and Greeks look for wisdom, but we preach Christ crucified: a stumbling block to Jews and foolishness to Gentiles, but to those whom God has called, both Jews and Greeks, Christ the power of God and the wisdom of God.

I resolved to nothing while I was with you except Jesus Christ and him crucified.

1 Corinthians 1:22-24; 2:2

34 Coming Again

Mosie Lister | Mosie Lister

C G6 G7 G9 F/C C
1. Je - sus is com - ing; Je - sus is com - ing;
2. In clouds of glo - ry, Bright clouds of glo - ry,
3. We'll rise to meet Him, Rise up to meet Him;
4. We shall be like Him; We shall be like Him;
5. O hal - le - lu - jah! O hal - le - lu - jah!

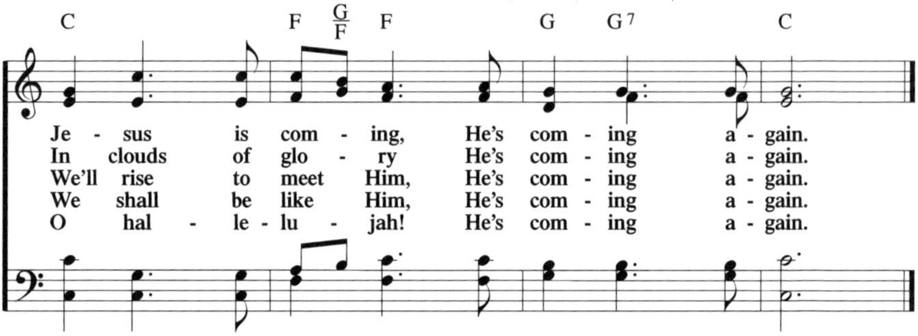
C F G/F F G G7 C
Je - sus is com - ing, He's com - ing a - gain.
In clouds of glo - ry He's com - ing a - gain.
We'll rise to meet Him, He's com - ing a - gain.
We shall be like Him, He's com - ing a - gain.
O hal - le - lu - jah! He's com - ing a - gain.

35 THE CROSS MADE THE DIFFERENCE

A Hymn Sequence

The Old Rugged Cross
The Old Rugged Cross Made the Difference

36 The Old Rugged Cross

George Bennard | George Bennard

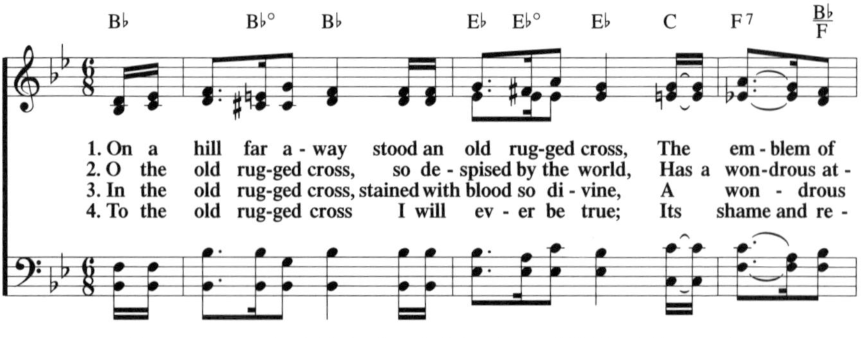
B♭ B♭° B♭ E♭ E♭° E♭ C F7 B♭/F
1. On a hill far a - way stood an old rug-ged cross, The em - blem of
2. O the old rug-ged cross, so de - spised by the world, Has a won-drous at -
3. In the old rug-ged cross, stained with blood so di - vine, A won - drous
4. To the old rug-ged cross I will ev - er be true; Its shame and re -

F7 B♭ B♭sus B♭ B♭° B♭ E♭ E♭° E♭
suf - f'ring and shame; And I love that old cross, where the dear - est and best
trac - tion for me; For the dear Lamb of God left His glo - ry a - bove
beau - ty I see; For 'twas on that old cross Je - sus suf - fered and died
proach glad - ly bear. Then He'll call me some - day to my home far a - way,
REFRAIN
C F7 F9 B♭/F F7 B♭ F B♭/F F7
For a world of lost sin - ners was slain.
To bear it to dark Cal - va - ry.
To par - don and sanc - ti - fy me.
Where His glo - ry for - ev - er I'll share.
So I'll cher - ish the old rug - ged cross, the
B♭ B♭° E♭/B♭ B♭ B♭/D E♭ B♭
cross, Till my tro - phies at last I lay down. I will cling to the
old rug - ged cross,
B♭ E♭/G B♭ E♭ B♭/F F7 B♭/F F7 B♭
old rug - ged cross, And ex - change it some - day for a crown.
cross, the old rug - ged cross,

Optional transition to “The Old Rugged Cross Made the Difference”

B♭
B♭/A♭
G sus
G
C

37 The Old Rugged Cross Made the Difference

William J. and Gloria Gaither

William J. Gaither

C
C sus
C
C7
C7/E
F
C
1. ’Twas a life filled with aim - less des-per - a - tion; With-out
2. There’s a room filled with sad, ash-en fac - es, With-out
C
F/C
C
Dm/C
C
G
D7/A
G7
Em/G
G7
hope walked the shell of a man. Then a
hope; death has wrapped them in gloom. But at the
C
C9
C7
C7/E
Gm/D
F
hand with a nail - print stretched down - ward; Just one
side of a saint there’s re - joic - ing, For

REFRAIN
touch, then a new life be - gan.
life can't be sealed in a tomb.
And the
old rug-ged cross made the dif - f'rence
In a life bound for
heart-ache and de - feat.
I will praise Him for - ev - er and
ev - er,
For the cross made the dif-f'rence for me.

End of Hymn Sequence "THE CROSS MADE THE DIFFERENCE"

God was pleased to have all his fullness dwell in him, and through him to reconcile to himself all things...by making peace through his blood, shed on the cross.

Once you were alienated from God...but now he has reconciled you by Christ's physical body through death to present you holy in his sight, without blemish and free from accusation.

Colossians 1:19-22

38 All That Thrills My Soul

Thoro Harris

Thoro Harris

1. Who can cheer the heart like Je - sus, By His pres - ence all di - vine?
2. Love of Christ so free - ly giv - en, Grace of God be - yond de - gree,
3. What a won - der - ful re - demp - tion! Nev - er can a mor - tal know
4. Ev - ery need His hand sup - ply - ing, Ev - ery good in Him I see;
5. By the crys - tal, flow - ing riv - er, With the ran - somed I will sing,
True and ten - der, pure and pre - cious, O how blest to call Him mine!
Mer - cy high - er than the heav - en, Deep - er than the deep - est sea!
How my sin, tho' red like crim - son, Can be whit - er than the snow.
On His strength di - vine re - ly - ing, He is All in All to me.
And for - ev - er and for - ev - er Praise and glo - ri - fy the King.
REFRAIN
All that thrills my soul is Je - sus; He is more than life to me.
to me.
And the fair - est of ten thou - sand In my bless - ed Lord I see.

The Longer I Serve Him

William J. Gaither

William J. Gaither

1. Since I start - ed for the King-dom, Since my life He con - trols,
2. Ev - ery need He is sup - ply - ing; Plen-teous grace He be - stows.
Since I gave my heart to Je - sus, The long - er I serve Him, the
Ev - ery day my way gets bright-er; The long - er I serve Him, the
sweet - er He grows.
sweet - er He grows.
REFRAIN
The long - er I serve Him, the sweet - er He grows. The
more that I love Him, more love He be - stows. Each day is like heav - en, my
heart o - ver - flows. The long - er I serve Him, the sweet - er He grows.

40 Just a Little Talk with Jesus

Cleavant Derricks

Cleavant Derricks

B♭ B♭+/D E♭ B♭
1. I once was lost in sin but Je - sus took me in, And
2. Some - times my path seems drear, with - out a ray of cheer, And
3. I may have doubts and fears, my eyes be filled with tears, But
B♭/D F B♭ F/A C7/G F C7/G F7
then a lit - tle light from heav - en filled my soul; It
then a cloud of doubt may hide the light of day; The
Je - sus is a friend who watch - es day and night; I
B♭ B♭+/D E♭ B♭
bathed my heart in love and wrote my name a - bove, And
mists of sin may rise and hide the star - ry skies, But
go to Him in prayer, He knows my ev - ery care, And
Gm B♭+ E♭m6/G♭ B♭/F F7 B♭ E♭/B♭ B♭
just a lit - tle talk with Je - sus makes me whole.
just a lit - tle talk with Je - sus clears the way.
just a lit - tle talk with Je - sus makes it right.
REFRAIN
Now let us

B♭ E♭/B♭ B♭ E♭/B♭ B♭
Have a lit-tle talk with Je-sus, tell Him all a-bout our trou-bles,
let us He will
F C7/G F7 B♭
Hear our faint-est cry, an-swer by and by;
and He will Now when you
E♭ B♭
Feel a lit-tle pray'r wheel turn-ing, know a lit-tle fire is burn-ing.
and you You will
Gm B♭+/G♭ E♭m6/G♭ B♭/F F7 B♭ E♭/B♭ B♭
Find a lit-tle talk with Je-sus makes it right.
right, it makes it right.

41 To God Be the Glory

Fanny J. Crosby

William H. Doane

1. To God be the glo - ry– great things He hath done: So loved He the
2. O per - fect re - demp-tion, the pur - chase of blood– To ev - ery be -
3. Great things He hath taught us, great things He hath done, And great our re -
world that He gave us His Son, Who yield - ed His life an a -
liev - er, the prom - ise of God! The vil - est of - fend - er who
joic - ing thro' Je - sus, the Son! But pur - er and high - er and
tone-ment for sin, And o - pened the life-gate that all may go in.
tru - ly be - lieves, That mo - ment from Je - sus a par - don re - ceives.
great - er will be Our won - der, our trans-port when Je - sus we see!
REFRAIN
Praise the Lord! Praise the Lord! Let the earth hear His voice! Praise the Lord!
Praise the Lord! Let the peo - ple re - joice! O come to the Fa - ther thro'

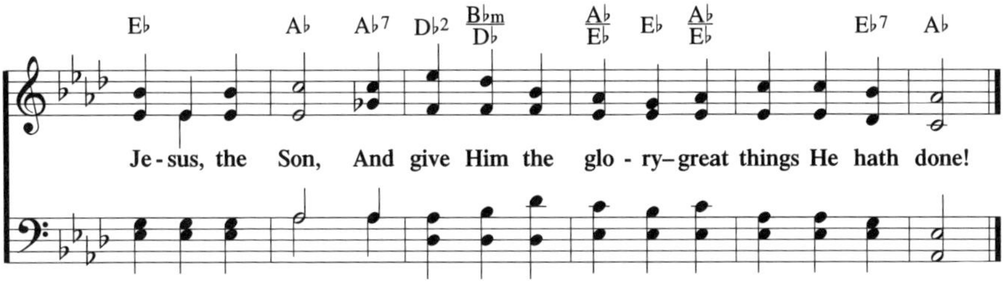
Je - sus, the Son, And give Him the glo - ry– great things He hath done!

Turn Your Eyes Upon Jesus

42

Helen H. Lemmel
and Ken Bible

Helen H. Lemmel

1. Turn your eyes up - on Je - sus, Look full in His won - der - ful face, And the things of earth will grow strange - ly dim In the light of His glo - ry and grace.
2. Turn you eyes up - on Je - sus, Take hold of His pow - er - ful hand. He will lift you up in His might - y love, In the strength of your God you can stand.

43 How Long Has It Been?

Mosie Lister

Mosie Lister

1. How long has it been since you talked with the Lord, And
2. How long has it been since you knelt by your bed And
told Him your heart's hid - den se - crets? How long since you
prayed to the Lord up in heav - en? How long since you
prayed? How long since you stayed On your knees 'til the light shone
knew that He'd an - swer you, And would keep you the long night
through? How long has it been since your mind felt at
through? How long has it been since you woke with the

A♭ C 7♯5 D♭ D♭° E♭/D♭ D♭ E♭/D♭ D♭ D♭/A♭ A♭
ease? How long since your heart knew no bur - den? Can you
dawn, And felt that the day's worth the liv - ing? Can you
D♭ D♭7 C 7 Fm B♭ B♭7/F
call Him your Friend? How long has it been Since you
call Him your Friend? How long has it been Since you
A♭/E♭ Cm/E♭ E♭7 A♭ A♭° D♭/A♭ A♭
knew that He cared for you?
knew that He cared for you?

"Ask and it will be given to you; seek and you will find; knock and the door will be opened to you. For everyone who asks receives; he who seeks finds; and to him who knocks, the door will be opened.

"Which of you fathers, if your son asks for a fish, will give him a snake instead? Or if he asks for an egg, will give him a scorpion?

"If you then, though you are evil, know how to give good gifts to your children, how much more will your Father in heaven give the Holy Spirit to those who ask him!"

Luke 11: 9-13

44 He'll Understand and Say, "Well Done"

Lucy E. Campbell
Ken Bible

Lucy E. Campbell

C C° C F G/F F C G7 C/G G7
1. If when you give the best of your ser - vice, Tell - ing the
2. When you are tried, so weak and dis - cour - aged, Turn to the
3. Tri - als will pass, they soon will be o - ver, Pain will be
G G7 G9 G6/A G7/B C C° C F G/F F
world that the Sav - ior has come. Be not dis - mayed when men don't be -
cross– see the Fa - ther's own Son. Look up in love and say with your
gone and the glo - ry be - gun. Then we will see the King in His
C F G/F F C/G F/G C/G G7 C
lieve you, He un - der - stands; He'll say, "Well done."
Sav - ior, "Not my own will, but Yours be done."
beau - ty, Bow - ing, we'll hear, "My child, well done."
REFRAIN
G7 C/G G7 G G7 G9 C/G G7 C G7 C/G G7
O when I come to the end of my jour - ney, Wear - y of
G G7 G9 G6/A G7/B C C° C C7/E F G/F F
life, and the bat - tle is won; Bear - ing the staff and cross of re -

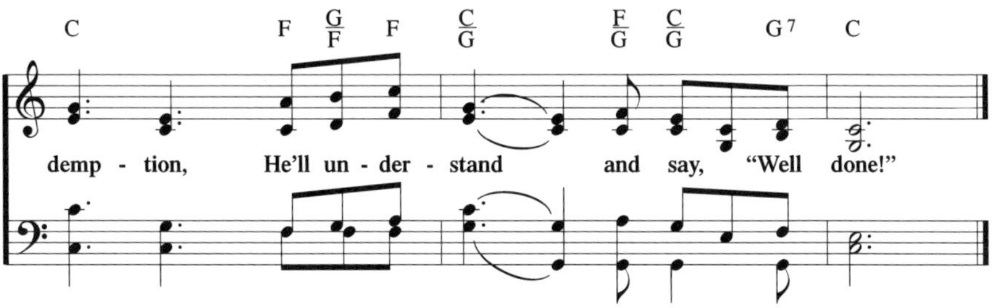
demp - tion, He'll un - der - stand and say, "Well done!"

Precious Lord, Take My Hand

45

Thomas A. Dorsey

George N. Allen
arranged by Thomas A. Dorsey

1. Pre - cious Lord, take my hand, Lead me on, help me stand. I am
2. When my way grows drear, Pre-cious Lord, lin - ger near– When my
3. When the dark - ness ap - pears And the night draws near, And the
tired, I am weak, I am worn. Thro' the storm, thro' the night, Lead me
life is al - most gone. Hear my cry, hear my call, Hold my
day is past and gone, At the riv - er I stand; Guide my
on to the light. Take my hand, pre-cious Lord; lead me home.
hand lest I fall. Take my hand, pre-cious Lord; lead me home.
feet, hold my hand. Take my hand, pre-cious Lord; lead me home.

46 Holy Savior

Mosie Lister

Mosie Lister
Arranged by Marty Parks

B♭ Cm/B♭ B♭M7 E♭ B♭ F7 B♭
Ho - ly Sav - ior, Lord, we a - dore You.
E♭ F/E♭ E♭ B♭ F F7 B♭
Ho - ly Sav - ior, Je - sus, Son of God.

47 CALVARY'S LOVE

A Hymn Sequence

Written in Red
My Savior's Love

48 Written in Red

Gordon Jensen

Gordon Jensen
Arranged by Marty Parks

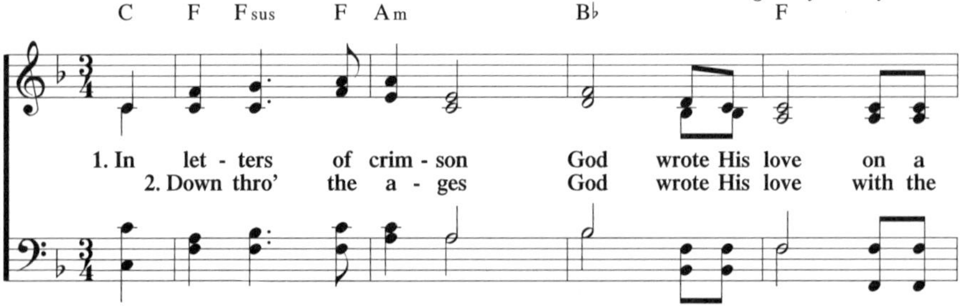
C F Fsus F Am B♭ F
1. In let - ters of crim - son God wrote His love on a
2. Down thro' the a - ges God wrote His love with the

hill - side so long, long a - go; For you and for me
same hands that suf - fered and bled; Giv - ing all He
Je - sus died, and love's great - est sto - ry was told.
had to give, a mes - sage so eas - i - ly read.
REFRAIN
I love you, I love you; That's what Cal - va-ry said. I
love you, I love you; I love you, writ-ten in red.

Optional transition to "My Savior's Love"

49 My Savior's Love

Charles H. Gabriel | Charles H. Gabriel

1. I stand a-mazed in the pres - ence Of Je - sus, the Naz - a - rene,
2. For me it was in the gar - den He prayed, "Not My will, but Thine."
3. In pit - y an - gels be-held Him And came from the world of light
4. He took my sins and my sor - rows, He made them His ver - y own;
5. When with the ran-somed in glo - ry His face I at last shall see,
And won-der how He could love me, A sin - ner, con-demned, un-clean.
He had no tears for His own griefs, But sweat-drops of blood for mine.
To com-fort Him in the sor - rows He bore for my soul that night.
He bore the bur - den to Cal - v'ry, And suf - fered and died a - lone.
'Twill be my joy thro' the a - ges To sing of His love for me.
REFRAIN
How mar-vel-ous! How won-der-ful!
O how mar-vel-ous! O how won-der-ful!
And my song shall ev - er be:
How mar-vel-ous! How won-der-ful
O how mar-vel-ous! O how won-der-ful!
Is my Sav-ior's love for me!

End of Hymn Sequence "CALVARY'S LOVE"

Love Is Why

Vep Ellis
W.F. Lakey

David Ellis
Vep Ellis

1. He never said I'd have silver or gold, Yet He has promised me
2. I was astray full of sin with it's shame, There was no peace within,
3. Tho' I have none of this worlds precious goods, Yet I'm an heir to all
riches untold; He never suffered a life without care, Yet He re-
I was to blame; Tho' undeserving, my life so defiled, Now to my
Heaven affords; Tho' I may never achieve earthly fame, Yet all of
lieves every burden I bear.
God I have been reconciled.
Heaven can call me by name.
REFRAIN
Sin stained the cross with the blood of my Lord;
Yet He permitted it without a word;
Why, tell me why He redeemed you and me?
Love is why you and I are free.

51 Ten Thousand Angels

Ray Overholt | Ray Overholt

1. They bound the hands of Je - sus in the gar - den where He prayed, They
2. Up - on His pre - cious head they placed a crown of thorns, They
3. When they nailed Him to the cross, His moth - er stood near - by, He
4. To the howl - ing mob He yield - ed, He did not for mer - cy cry; The
led Him thro' the streets in shame. The spat up - on the Sav - ior so
laughed and said, "Be - hold the King." They struck Him and they cursed Him and
said, "Wom - an, be - hold thy son!" He cried, "I thirst for wa - ter," but they
cross of shame He took a - lone. And when He cried, "It's fin - ished!" He
pure and free from sin, They said, "Cru - ci - fy Him! He's to blame!"
mocked His ho - ly name, All a - lone He suf - fered ev - ery - thing.
gave Him none to drink. Then the sin - ful work of man was done.
gave him - self to die; Sal - va - tion's won - drous plan was done.
REFRAIN
He could have called ten thou - sand an - gels To de - stroy the

B♭7/F B♭7 B♭ Gm/B♭ B♭9 E♭ B♭7/F E♭ Fm7 E♭7/G A♭ E♭M7(4)/A♭ A♭ A♭/C A♭
world and set Him free. He could have called ten thou-sand
E♭ B♭/F E♭/G B♭ B♭7 E♭
an - gels, But He died a - lone for you and me.
a - lone

While [Jesus] was still speaking, Judas, one of the Twelve, arrived. With him was a large crowd armed with swords and clubs, sent from the chief priests and the elders of the people. Now the betrayer had arranged a signal with them: "The one I kiss is the man; arrest him." Going at once to Jesus, Judas said, "Greetings, Rabbi!" and kissed him.

Jesus replied, "Friend, do what you came for."

Then the men stepped forward, seized Jesus and arrested him. With that, one of Jesus' companions reached for his sword, drew it out and struck the servant of the high priest, cutting off his ear.

"Put your sword back in its place," Jesus said to him, "for all who draw the sword will die by the sword. Do you think I cannot call on my Father, and he will at once put at my disposal more than twelve legions of angels? But how then would the Scriptures be fulfilled that say it must happen in this way?"

Matthew 26:47-54

52 If That Isn't Love

Dottie Rambo — Dottie Rambo

1. He left the splen - dor of heav - en,
2. E - ven in death He re - mem - bered The
Know - ing His des - ti - ny Was the
thief hang - ing by His side. He
lone - ly hill of Gol - goth - a; There to
spoke with love and com - pas - sion; Then He
lay down His life for me.
took him to Par - a - dise. If
REFRAIN
that is - n't love the o - cean is

B♭ E♭/B♭ B♭ F7
dry, There's no stars in the sky,
F9 Dm/F E♭/F B♭
and the spar - row can't fly! If
B♭9 B♭7 B♭7/D E♭ Cm/E♭ E♭
that is - n't love then heav - en's a
B♭ E♭/B♭ B♭ F7
myth. There's no feel - ing like this,
F7 Dm/F F9 Dm/F F7 B♭ E♭/B♭ B♭
if that is - n't love.

53 He Has Surely Borne Our Sorrow

Mosie Lister | Mosie Lister

1. Once on a cross there hung in sor - row One who was will-ing to
2. See on His brow the scars the thorns made; See where the spear was
3. There is no death, for He has ris - en. Death and the grace have been
die for our sins; God's on - ly Son, sent down from heav - en,
thrust in His side; See in His hand where nails were driv - en,
con-quered at last; And this I know– we shall be like Him
Came to re - deem all men.
Oh, how He suf-fered and died!
In His own glo - ry at last.
REFRAIN
He has sure - ly borne our
sor - row; He has tak - en the sin-debt a - way. He was
bruised for our trans-gres - sions, And by His stripes we are healed to - day.
Song ending

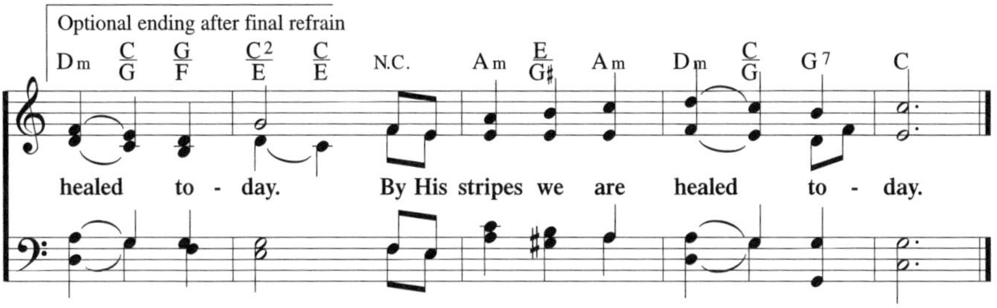
Optional ending after final refrain
Dm C/G G/F C2/E C/E N.C. Am E/G♯ Am Dm C/G G7 C
healed to - day. By His stripes we are healed to - day.

All the Glory Belongs to Jesus

54

Gloria Gaither

William J. Gaither

C G C G7/D C/E F Em7 Dm7 C G/B Am7 G
All the glo - ry be - longs to Je - sus. All the praise
G Gm Gm7 C7 C Dm7 C/E F FM7 G9/F
be - longs to Him. All that I am or ev - er
C2/E C G/D C/E D7sus G7sus F/G C
hope to be, All the glo - ry be - longs to Him.

55 He Looked Beyond My Fault

Dottie Rambo

Adapted from *Londonderry Aire*
Arranged by Marty Parks

A - maz - ing Grace shall al - ways be my song of praise,
For it was grace that bought my lib - er - ty.
I do not know just why He came to love me so;
He looked be - yond my fault and saw my need.
REFRAIN
I shall for - ev - er lift mine eyes to Cal - va - ry

C G9 E/G♯ Am Em G/F F C Dm7 G7
To view the cross where Je - sus died for me.
Gsus G C E7♯5 F6 F C E/G♯ Am
How mar - vel - ous the grace that caught my fall - ing soul;
Em/G Fm/A♭ Fm6/A♭ C/G F/G C/G Dm Dm7 F/G G7 C
He looked be - yond my fault and saw my need.

At just the right time, when we were still powerless, Christ died for the ungodly. Very rarely will anyone die for a righteous man, though for a good man someone might possibly dare to die.

But God demonstrates his own love for us in this: While we were still sinners, Christ died for us.

Romans 5:6-8

56 Take Me to the Fountain

Mosie Lister

Mosie Lister

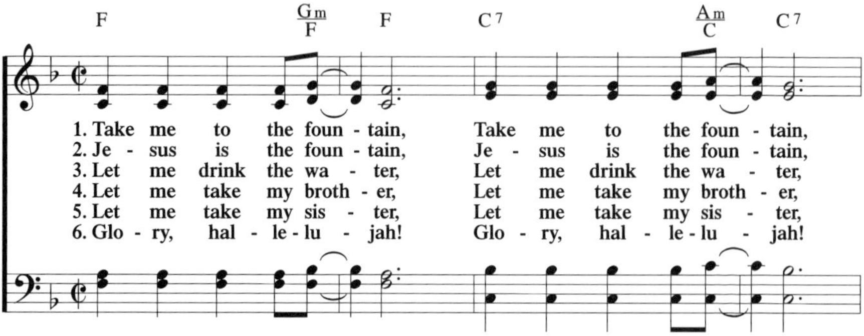
F Gm/F F C7 Am/C C7
1. Take me to the foun - tain, Take me to the foun - tain,
2. Je - sus is the foun - tain, Je - sus is the foun - tain,
3. Let me drink the wa - ter, Let me drink the wa - ter,
4. Let me take my broth - er, Let me take my broth - er,
5. Let me take my sis - ter, Let me take my sis - ter,
6. Glo - ry, hal - le - lu - jah! Glo - ry, hal - le - lu - jah!

F F7 Cm/B♭ B♭ Gm/B♭ F/C C7 F
To the liv - ing foun - tain That nev - er shall run dry.
He's the liv - ing foun - tain, That nev - er shall run dry.
From the liv - ing foun - tain That nev - er shall run dry.
To the liv - ing foun - tain That nev - er shall run dry.
To the liv - ing foun - tain That nev - er shall run dry.
For the liv - ing foun - tain That nev - er shall run dry.

57 CALVARY

A Hymn Sequence

At the Cross
At Calvary

58 At the Cross

Isaac Watts
ref.,Ralph E. Hudson

Ralph E. Hudson

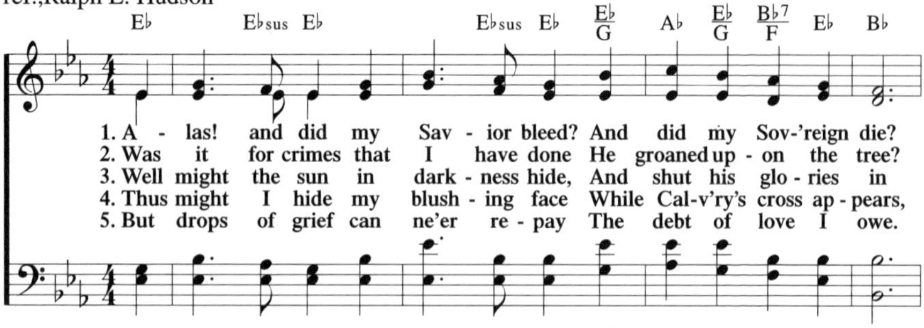
E♭ E♭sus E♭ E♭sus E♭ E♭/G A♭ E♭/G B♭7/F E♭ B♭
1. A - las! and did my Sav - ior bleed? And did my Sov-'reign die?
2. Was it for crimes that I have done He groaned up - on the tree?
3. Well might the sun in dark - ness hide, And shut his glo - ries in
4. Thus might I hide my blush - ing face While Cal-v'ry's cross ap - pears,
5. But drops of grief can ne'er re - pay The debt of love I owe.

Would He de - vote that sa - cred head For sin - ners such as I?
A - maz - ing pit - y! grace un-known! And love be - yond de - gree!
When Christ, the might - y Mak - er, died For man, the crea-ture's, sin.
Dis - solve my heart in thank - ful - ness, And melt mine eyes to tears.
Here, Lord, I give my - self a - way; 'Tis all that I can do.
REFRAIN
At the cross, at the cross, where I first saw the light, And the
bur - den of my heart rolled a - way.
rolled a - way.
It was there by
faith I re - ceived my sight, And now I am hap-py all the day!
Optional transition to "At Calvary"

59 At Calvary

William R. Newell

Daniel B. Towner

1. Years I spent in van - i - ty and pride, Car - ing not my Lord was cru - ci - fied,
2. By God's Word at last my sin I learned; Then I trem-bled at the law I'd spurned,
3. Now I've giv'n to Je - sus ev - ery-thing; Now I glad - ly own Him as my King;
4. O the love that drew sal - va-tion's plan! O the grace that bro't it down to man!
Know - ing not it was for me He died On Cal - va - ry.
Till my guilt - y soul im - plor - ing turned To Cal - va - ry.
Now my rap - tured soul can on - ly sing Of Cal - va - ry.
O the might - y gulf that God did span At Cal - va - ry!
REFRAIN
Mer - cy there was great and grace was free; Par - don there was mul - ti - plied to me;
There my bur - dened soul found lib - er - ty, At Cal - va - ry.

End of Hymn Sequence "CALVARY"

Wonderful Savior

J. D. Sumner

J. D. Sumner

1. I have start - ed out to fol-low Je - sus, Ev-ery day, ev - ery hour I want to be Just a lit - tle more like my bless - ed Je - sus; He means more than all the world to me.
2. In His foot - steps I will al - way fol - low; In His ev - er gra - cious pres - ence I would be. Tho' the storms of life may rage, my Lord will guide me. What a kind and faith - ful Sav - ior is He.
REFRAIN
Oh, won - der - ful, won - der - ful is Je - sus. He gave His life on cru - el Cal - va - ry. He'll be there when I start to cross the Jor - dan; What a won - der - ful Sav - ior is He.

61 Hallelujah! We Shall Rise

J. E. Thomas J. E. Thomas

1. In that re - sur - rec - tion morn - ing When the trump of God shall sound,
2. In that re - sur - rec - tion morn - ing, What a meet - ing it will be,
3. In that re - sur - rec - tion morn - ing, Bless - ed tho't it is to me,
4. In that re - sur - rec - tion morn - ing We shall meet Him in the air,
We shall rise, we shall rise!
Hal - le - lu - jah!
Then the
When our
I shall
And be
saints will come re - joic - ing, And no tears will e'er be found,
fa - thers and our moth - ers, And our loved ones we shall see,
see my bless - ed Sav - ior Who so free - ly died for me,
car - ried up to glo - ry To our home so bright and fair,
We shall
rise, we shall rise!
Hal - le - lu - jah! in that morn - ing we shall rise.
REFRAIN
We shall
N.C.
Fm
Eb7
Ab
Absus

Hal - le-lu-jah! A - men! We shall rise! In the
rise, we shall rise! Hal - le-lu-jah!
res - ur - rec - tion morn-ing When death's pris - on bars are bro - ken, We shall
rise, we shall rise!
Hal - le - lu - jah! in that morn-ing we shall rise.

According to the Lord's own word, we tell you that we who are still alive, who are left till the coming of the Lord, will certainly not precede those who have fallen asleep.

For the Lord himself will come down from heaven, with a loud command, with the voice of the archangel and with the trumpet call of God, and the dead in Christ will rise first.

After that, we who are still alive and are left will be caught up together with them in the clouds to meet the Lord in the air. And so we will be with the Lord forever. Therefore encourage each other with these words.

1 Thessalonians 4:15-18

62 Mansion Over the Hilltop

Ira F. Stanphill Ira F. Stanphill

C Dm/C B/C C C/E F C A°7
1. I'm sat - is - fied with just a cot-tage be - low, A lit - tle
2. Tho' oft - en temp - ted, tor - ment-ed and test - ed And, like the
3. Don't think me poor or de - sert-ed or lone - ly– I'm not dis -
G7 G°7 C Dm/C B/C C C/E
sil - ver and a lit - tle gold; But in that cit - y where the
proph - et, my pil-low a stone; And tho' I find here no
cour - aged, I'm Heav - en bound; I'm just a pil - grim in
F C Em/G F/G F♯/G G G9 Em/G G C F/C C
ran-somed will shine, I want a gold one that's sil - ver - lined.
per - ma - nent dwell-ing, I know He'll give me a man-sion my own.
search of a cit - y, I want a man-sion, a harp and a crown.
REFRAIN
C G7sus/D C/E F C Em/G F/G F♯/G
I've got a man - sion just o - ver the hill - top, In that bright

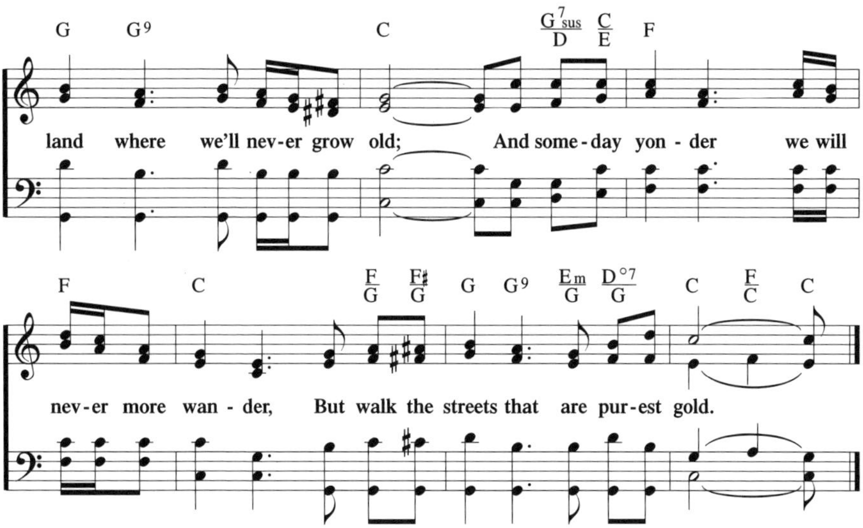
land where we'll nev-er grow old; And some-day yon-der we will
nev-er more wan-der, But walk the streets that are pur-est gold.

Only Believe

63

Paul Rader

Paul Rader

On-ly be-lieve, on-ly be-lieve; All things are
pos-si-ble, on-ly be-lieve. On-ly be-lieve, on-ly be-
lieve; All things are pos-si-ble, on-ly be-lieve.

64 I'm Feeling Fine

Mosie Lister — Mosie Lister

1. Well, I woke up this morn-ing feel-ing fine; I woke up with heav-en on my
2. I've been walk-ing with Je-sus all the time; We're walk-ing and talk-ing as we
mind. I woke up with joy in my soul, 'Cause I knew my Lord had con-trol.
climb. We're trav-'ling a road to the sky Where I know I'll live when I die.
Well, I knew I was walk-ing in the light, 'Cause I'd been on my knees in the
He's been tell-ing me all a-bout that land, And He tells me that ev-ery-thing is
night, And I'd prayed 'till the Lord gave a sign, And now I'm feel-ing might-y fine.
grand; And He says that a home will be mine, And now I'm feel-ing might-y fine.
REFRAIN
Well, I'm feel-ing, feel-ing might-y fine, I've got
Feel-ing might-y fine, yes, I'm feel-ing fine.

C7 F B♭7
heav-en on my mind. Don't you know I want to
Heav-en on my mind, heav-en on my mind. Oh, I want to go,
F G7 C7
go Where the milk and hon-ey flow. There's a
yes, I want to go, milk and hon-ey flow, milk and hon-ey flow.
F C7/G C7
light that al-ways shines Down in-side
Light that al-ways shines, light that al-ways shines, In this heart of
C7 F B♭ B♭7
this heart of mine. I've got heav-en, heav-en on my
mine, in this heart of mine. Heav-en on my mind,
F C7 F B♭ F
mind. And I'm feel-ing, feel-ing might-y fine.
heav-en on my mind, Feel-ing might-y fine, yes, I'm feel-ing fine.

65 The Eastern Gate

Isaiah G. Martin | Isaiah G. Martin

1. I will meet you in the morn-ing, Just in-side the East-ern Gate.
2. If you has-ten off to glo-ry, Lin-ger near the East-ern Gate,
3. Keep your lamps all trimmed and burn-ing; For the Bride-groom watch and wait.
4. O the joys of that glad meet-ing With the saints who for us wait!
Then be read-y, faith-ful pil-grim, Lest with you it be too late.
For I'm com-ing in the morn-ing; So you'll not have long to wait.
He'll be with us at the meet-ing Just in-side the East-ern Gate.
What a bless-ed, hap-py meet-ing Just in-side the East-ern Gate.
REFRAIN
I will meet you, I will meet you Just in-
meet you in the morn-ing, meet you in the morn-ing,
side the East-ern Gate o-ver there.
o-ver there.
I will meet you,
meet you in the morn-ing,
I will meet you, I will meet you in the morn-ing o-ver there.
meet you in the morn-ing,

The Last Mile of the Way

Johnson Oatman, Jr. — William Edie Marks

1. If I walk in the path-way of du-ty, If I work till the close of the day; I shall see the great King in His beau-ty,
2. If for Christ I pro-claim the glad sto-ry, If I seek for His sheep gone a-stray, I am sure He will show me His glo-ry,
3. Here the dear-est of ties we must sev-er, Tears of sor-row are seen ev-ery day; But no sick-ness, no sigh-ing for-ev-er
4. And if here I have ear-nest-ly striv-en, And have tried all His will to o-bey, 'Twill en-hance all the rap-ture of heav-en,
REFRAIN
When I've gone the last mile of the way.
When I've gone the last mile of the way, I will rest at the close of the day;
the last mile of the way, at the close of the day;
And I know there are joys that a-wait me, When I've gone the last mile of the way.

67 BEULAH LAND

A Hymn Sequence

Sweet Beulah Land
When We All Get to Heaven

68 Sweet Beulah Land

Squire Parsons, Jr. Squire Parsons, Jr.

1. I'm kind of home - (kind of home -) sick for a coun-try
2. I'm look - ing now (look-ing now) a-cross the riv - er
To which I've nev - (where I've nev -) er been be - fore;
Where my faith (where my faith) will end in sight;
No sad good - bys (sad good - bys) will there be spo-ken,
There's just a few (just a few) more days to la - bor,
For time won't mat - (time won't mat -) ter an - y more.
Then I will take (I will take) my heav'n - ly flight.

REFRAIN
Beu - lah land, I'm long - ing for you,
And some-day on thee I'll stand;
There my home shall be e - ter - nal,
Beu - lah land, sweet Beu - lah land.

Optional transition to "When We All Get to Heaven"

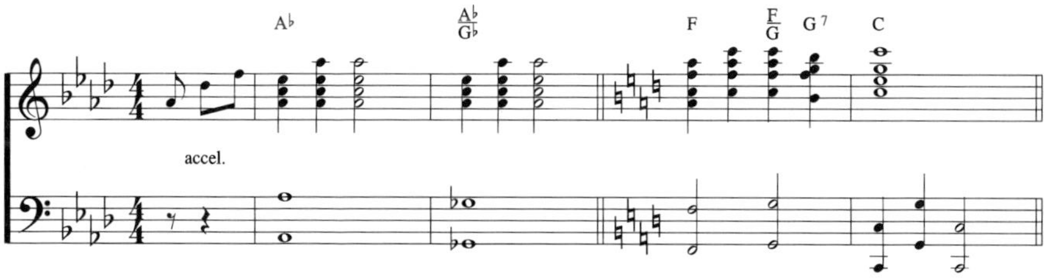
accel.

69 When We All Get to Heaven

Eliza E. Hewitt

Emily D. Wilson

C G7 C
1. Sing the won-drous love of Je - sus; Sing His mer - cy and His grace.
2. While we walk the pil - grim path-way, Clouds will o - ver - spread the sky;
3. Let us then be true and faith - ful, Trust - ing, serv - ing ev - ery day.
4. On - ward to the prize be - fore us! Soon His beau - ty we'll be - hold.
F F♯°7 C/G G7sus G9 C F/C C
In the man - sions, bright and bless - ed, He'll pre - pare for us a place.
But when trav - 'ling days are o - ver, Not a shad - ow, not a sigh!
Just one glimpse of Him in glo - ry Will the toils of life re - pay.
Soon the pearl - y gates will o - pen; We shall tread the streets of gold.
(1.) pare for us a place.
REFRAIN
C C/E
When we all get to heav - en, What a day of re -
When we all What a
D7 G7 C C7/E
joic - ing that will be! When we all see
day of re - joic - ing that will be! When we all
F F♯°7 C/G G sus G9 C F/C C
Je - sus, We'll sing and shout the vic - to - ry!
We'll sing and shout, and shout the vic - to - ry.

End of Hymn Sequence "BEULAH LAND"

At the Crossing

Mosie Lister

Mosie Lister

1. There's a riv - er some - where that's called Jor - dan, And they say that it's
2. Tho' the riv - er is dark and storm - y, It will pass like a
deep and it's wide; And they say that the King and the beg - gar On that
dream in the night; And my soul will a - wake in the morn-ing In
shore will stand side by side.
re - gions of end-less de - light.
At the cross-ing of the Jor - dan,
Why should I be a - fraid? There'll be Some - one there who loves me To
guide me 'cross the riv - er to end - less joys a - bove.

71 A New Name in Glory

C. Austin Miles C. Austin Miles

1. I was once a sin - ner, but I came Par - don to re - ceive from my
2. I was hum - bly kneel - ing at the cross, Fear - ing naught but God's an - gry
3. In the Book 'tis writ - ten, "Saved by grace." O the joy that came to my
Lord. This was free - ly giv - en, and I found That He al - ways kept His
frown, When the heav - ens o - pened and I saw That my name was writ - ten
soul! Now I am for - giv - en, and I know By the blood I am made
REFRAIN
word. (kept His word.)
down. (writ - ten down.) There's a new name writ - ten down in glo - ry, And it's
whole. (am made whole.)
mine, O yes, it's mine! And the white - robed an - gels sing the
And it's mine, yes, it's mine!
sto - ry, "A sin - ner has come home." For there's a
home, has come home."

A♭ B♭m/A♭ A♭ D♭ A♭
new name writ-ten down in glo-ry, And it's mine, O yes, it's mine!
And it's mine, yes, it's mine!
D♭ A♭ D♭ A♭/E♭ E♭7 E♭ A♭
With my sins for - giv-en I am bound for heav-en, Nev - er - more to roam.

Now the tax collectors and "sinners" were all gathering around to hear [Jesus]. But the Pharisees and the teachers of the law muttered, "This man welcomes sinners and eats with them."

Then Jesus told them this parable:

"Suppose one of you has a hundred sheep and loses one of them. Does he not leave the ninety-nine in the open country and go after the lost sheep until he finds it? And when he finds it, he joyfully puts it on his shoulders and goes home. Then he calls his friends and neighbors together and says, 'Rejoice with me; I have found my lost sheep.' I tell you that in the same way there will be more rejoicing in heaven over one sinner who repents than over ninety-nine righteous persons who do not need to repent."

Luke 15:1-7

72 Speak His Name

Mosie Lister
Mosie Lister

1. Speak His name and de - mons trem - ble, Speak His name and an - gels as - sem - ble. Speak His name and mul - ti - tudes bow in awe and rev-'rence be - fore His throne.
2. Speak His name when a loved one is dy - ing, Speak His name and the sad heart stops cry - ing; Speak His name and glad hearts sing to - geth - er, a - dor - ing be - fore His throne.
3. In His name is peace for the na - tions, In His name is hope of sal - va - tion; In His name the wan - der - er tossed and dri - ven finds com - fort and peace un - known.
REFRAIN
Je - sus, Je - sus, Name of our Lord whose praise we sing; Je - sus, Je - sus, Je - sus, our Lord and King.

There Is Power in the Blood

Lewis E. Jones

Lewis E. Jones

1. Would you be free from your bur - den of sin? There's pow'r in the blood,
2. Would you be free from your pas - sion and pride? There's pow'r in the blood,
3. Would you be whit - er, much whit - er than snow? There's pow'r in the blood,
4. Would you do ser - vice for Je - sus, your King? There's pow'r in the blood,
pow'r in the blood; Would you o'er e - vil a vic - to - ry win? There's
pow'r in the blood; Come for a cleans - ing to Cal - va - ry's tide. There's
pow'r in the blood; Sin - stains are lost in its life - giv - ing flow. There's
pow'r in the blood; Would you live dai - ly His prais - es to sing? There's
won - der - ful pow'r in the blood.
REFRAIN
There is pow'r, pow'r, won - der - work - ing
There is pow'r, there is pow'r, won - der - work - ing
pow'r In the blood of the Lamb. There is pow'r, pow'r,
pow'r In the blood of the Lamb. There is pow'r, there is pow'r,
won - der - work - ing pow'r In the pre - cious blood of the Lamb.

74 The Happy Jubilee

Raymond Browning — Adger M. Pace

B♭ D7 E♭ B♭
1. Praise the Lord, I've been in - vit - ed to a meet - ing in the air,
2. With the glo - ri - ous as - sem - bly dressed in gar - ments pure and white,
3. Sa - tan will be bound and wars will cease and Da - vid's Son will reign,
B♭ F7 B♭
Ju - bi - lee! Ju - bi - lee!
Ju - bi - lee! Ju - bi - lee!
B♭ D7 E♭ B♭
All the saints of all the a - ges in their glo - ry will be there;
You will find me, for I'm watch - ing and my lamp is trimmed and bright;
All the ran - somed of the Lord shall come to Zi - on once a - gain.
B♭ E♭ Cm B♭/F F7 B♭ E♭/B♭ E♭
Oh, I'm go - ing to that hap - py ju - bi - lee!
Oh, I'm go - ing to that hap - py ju - bi - lee!
And I'm go - ing to that hap - py ju - bi - lee! ju - bi - lee!

REFRAIN
N.C.
E♭
B♭
B♭/D
F
Ju - bi-lee! Ju - bi - lee! I am
Ju - bi - lee! Ju - bi - lee!
B♭
F/A
Gm
C7
F
F7
go - ing to that hap-py ju - bi - lee!
ju - bi - lee!
N.C.
E♭
B♭
B♭/D
F
Ju - bi - lee! Ju - bi - lee! Yes, I'm
Ju - bi - lee! Ju - bi - lee!
B♭
F/A
Gm
F7
B♭
E♭/B♭
E♭
go - ing to that hap-py ju - bi - lee!
ju - bi - lee!

75 We'll Understand It Better By and By

Charles A. Tindley Charles A. Tindley

1. Tri-als dark on ev-ery hand, And we can-not un-der-stand
2. Oft our cher-ished plans have failed, Dis-ap-point-ments have pre-vailed,
3. Temp-ta-tions, hid-den snares Of-ten take us un-a-wares,
All the ways that God would lead us to that bless-ed Prom-ised Land;
And we've wan-dered in the dark-ness, heav-y-heart-ed and a-lone;
And our hearts are made to bleed for some tho't-less word or deed,
But He'll guide us with His eye, And we'll fol-low till we die; We will
But we're trust-ing in the Lord, And, ac-cord-ing to His Word, We will
And we won-der why the test When we try to do our best, But we'll
un-der-stand it bet-ter by and by.
REFRAIN
By and by, when the morn-ing comes,

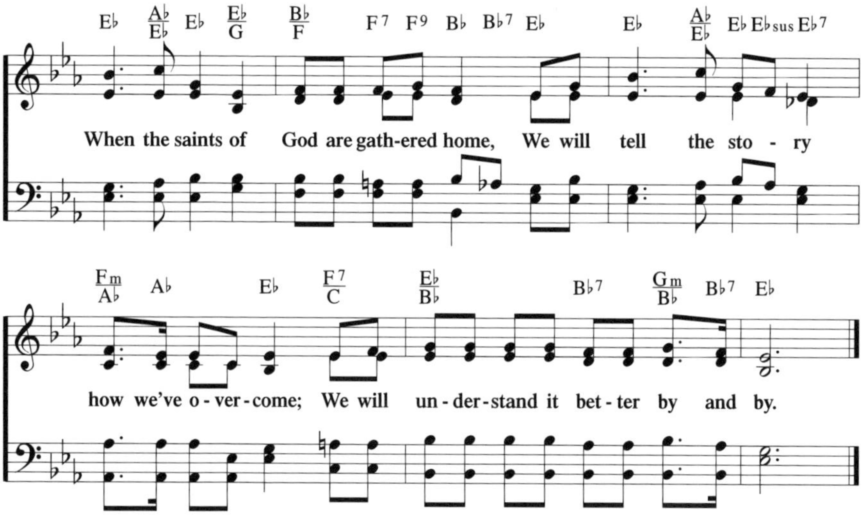
E♭ A♭/E♭ E♭ E♭/G B♭/F F7 F9 B♭ B♭7 E♭ E♭ A♭/E♭ E♭ E♭sus E♭7
When the saints of God are gath-ered home, We will tell the sto - ry
Fm/A♭ A♭ E♭ F7/C E♭/B♭ B♭7 Gm/B♭ B♭7 E♭
how we've o - ver - come; We will un - der - stand it bet - ter by and by.

Learning to Lean

76

John Stallings

John Stallings
Arranged by Marty Parks

F B♭/F F Gm/B♭ B♭ F F/E♭
Learn - ing to lean, learn - ing to lean; I'm learn - ing to
D7 G9 Csus C7 F B♭/F F7 E♭/F F7 Gm/B♭ B♭
lean on Je - sus. Find - ing more pow - er than I'd ev - er
B♭ F F/E♭ D7 G G7 C7 F
dreamed; I'm learn - ing to lean on Je - sus.

77

'Til the Storm Passes By

Mosie Lister | Mosie Lister

D♭ D♭sus D♭ D♭sus D♭ A♭7 A♭° A♭7
1. In the dark of the mid-night Have I oft hid my face,
2. Man - y times Sa - tan whis-pered, "There is no need to try,
3. When the long night has end - ed, And the storms come no more,
A♭7 G♭/A♭ A♭ G♭/A♭ Fm/A♭ A♭ G♭/A♭ Fm/A♭ A♭7 E♭m7 A♭/C A♭7/C D♭
While the storm howls a - bove me, And there's no hid - ing place.
For there's no end of sor - row; There's no hope by and by."
Let me stand in Thy pres - ence On that bright, peace-ful shore.
D♭ D♭sus D♭ D♭sus D♭ D♭7sus D♭7 G♭ G♭sus G♭
'Mid the crash of the thun-der, Pre - cious Lord, hear my cry,
But I know Thou art with me, And to - mor - row I'll rise
In that land where the tem-pest Nev - er comes, Lord, may I
G♭ D♭ B♭m E♭m/B♭ D♭/A♭ A♭7 D♭ REFRAIN A♭ D♭/A♭
"Keep me safe 'til the storm pass-es by."
Where the storm nev - er dark - ens the skies. 'Til the storm pass - es
Dwell with Thee when the storm pass - es by.

A♭7 A♭ Fm/A♭ A♭7 D♭ D♭/F E♭7
o - ver, 'Til the thun - der sounds no more, 'Til the clouds roll for -
E♭7 Fm/E♭ E♭7 A♭ A♭/G♭ D♭/F D♭ D♭7
ev - er from the sky, Hold me fast, let me stand In the
E♭m/G♭ G♭ D♭ G♭/D♭ D♭ B♭m E♭7/B♭♭ D♭/A♭ A♭7 D♭
hol - low of Thy hand; Keep me safe 'til the storm pass - es by.

This is what the Lord says–
he who created you, O Jacob, he who formed you, O Israel:
"Fear not, for I have redeemed you;
I have summoned you by name; you are mine.
When you pass through the waters, I will be with you;
And when you pass through the rivers, they will not sweep over you.
When you walk through the fire, you will not be burned;
the flames will not set you ablaze.
For I am the Lord, your God, the Holy One of Israel, your Savior…
You are precious and honored in my sight…
I love you…
Do not be afraid, for I am with you.

Isaiah 43:1-5

78 Stand By Me

Charles A. Tindley — Charles A. Tindley

G Gsus G Bm/D D7 G/D C Am7 G C/G G
1. When the storms of life are rag-ing, stand by me.
2. In the midst of faults and fail-ures, stand by me.
3. When I'm grow-ing old and fee-ble, stand by me.
stand by me.
G D7 D9 G Em D G/D D7
When the storms of life are rag-ing, stand by me.
In the midst of faults and fail-ures, stand by me.
When I'm grow-ing old and fee-ble, stand by me.
stand by me.
D7 Em/G G Em/G G Em D G G/D Em7 Bm7
When the world is toss-ing me like a ship up-on the
When I do the best I can and my friends mis-un-der-
When my life be-comes a bur-den and I'm near-ing chill-y
A7 A7/E G/D Bm/D D7 G/D C Am7 G
sea; Thou who rul-est wind and wat-er, stand by me.
stand, Thou who know-est all a-bout me, stand by me.
Jor-dan; O Thou Lil-y of the Val-ley, stand by me.

GLORYLAND

A Hymn Sequence

I Feel Like Traveling On
Just Over in the Gloryland

I Feel like Traveling On

William Hunter

Anonymous

F
Fsus F
C/E G7/D C
1. My heav'n - ly home is bright and fair, I feel like trav-el-ing on.
2. Its glit - t'ring tow'rs the sun out-shine, I feel like trav-el-ing on.
3. Let oth - ers seek a home be-low– I feel like trav-el-ing on.
4. The Lord has been so good to me, I feel like trav-el-ing on.
F
Fsus F
F/C
C7 F
Nor pain, nor death can en - ter there, I feel like trav-el-ing on.
That heav'n - ly man - sion shall be mine, I feel like trav-el-ing on.
Which flames de - vour or waves o'er-flow, I feel like trav-el-ing on.
Un - til that bless - ed home I see, I feel like trav-el-ing on.
REFRAIN
F Fsus F
Fsus F
C F
C/E G7/D C
Yes, I feel like trav-el-ing on. I feel like trav-el-ing on.
Yes, I feel like trav-el-ing, trav-el-ing on. I feel like trav-el-ing, trav-el-ing on.
F
Fsus F
F/C
C7 F
My heav'n - ly home is bright and fair, I feel like trav-el-ing on.

Optional Transition to "Just Over In the Glory Land"

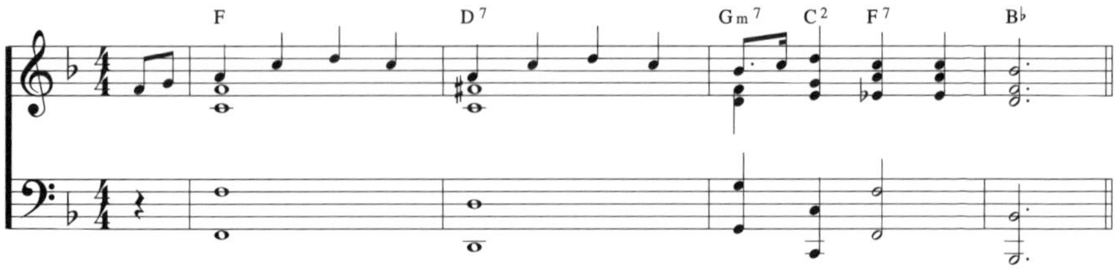
F D7 Gm7 C2 F7 B♭

81 Just Over in the Glory Land

James W. Acuff

Emmet S. Dean

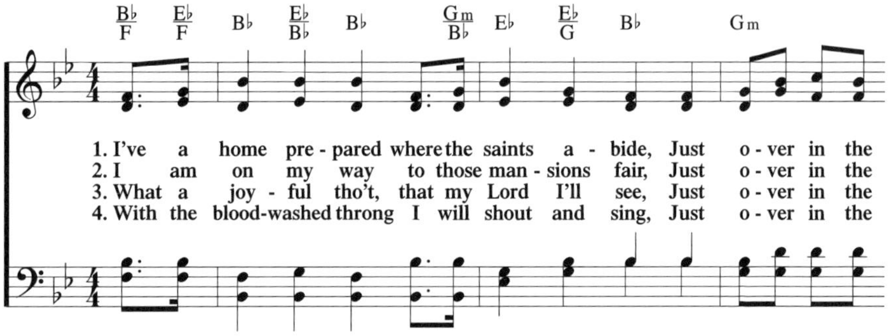
B♭/F E♭/F B♭ E♭/B♭ B♭ Gm/B♭ E♭ E♭/G B♭ Gm
1. I've a home prepared where the saints a - bide, Just o - ver in the
2. I am on my way to those man - sions fair, Just o - ver in the
3. What a joy - ful tho't, that my Lord I'll see, Just o - ver in the
4. With the blood-washed throng I will shout and sing, Just o - ver in the

C9 C7 F Dm/F E♭/F B♭ E♭/B♭ B♭ E♭ E♭/G B♭ Dm7/A
glo - ry land; And I long to be by my Sav - ior's side. Just
glo - ry land; There to sing God's praise and His glo - ry share, Just
glo - ry land; And with kin - dred saved, there for - ev - er be, Just
glo - ry land; Glad ho - san - nas to Christ the Lord and King, Just

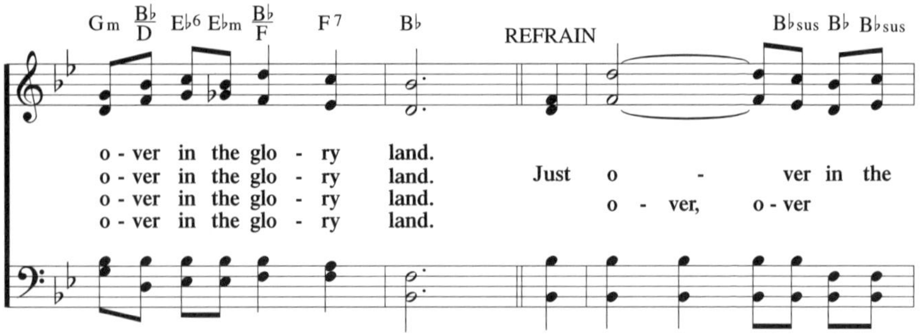
Gm B♭/D E♭6 E♭m B♭/F F7 B♭
REFRAIN
B♭sus B♭ B♭sus
o - ver in the glo - ry land.
o - ver in the glo - ry land.
o - ver in the glo - ry land.
o - ver in the glo - ry land.
Just o - ver in the
o - ver, o - ver

glo - ry land, I'll join the hap-py an - gel band, Just
join, yes, join
o - ver in the glo - ry land; Just o - ver in the glo - ry land,
o - ver, o - ver
There with the might - y host I'll stand, Just o - ver in the glo - ry land.
with, yes, with

End of Hymn Sequence "GLORYLAND"

Then I saw a new heaven and a new earth, for the first heaven and the first earth had passed away, and there was no longer any sea. I saw the Holy City, the new Jerusalem, coming down out of heaven from God, prepared as a bride beautifully dressed for her husband.

And I heard a loud voice from the throne saying, "Now the dwelling of God is with men, and he will live with them. They will be his people, and God himself will be with them and be their God. He will wipe every tear from their eyes. There will be no more death or mourning or crying or pain, for the old order of things has passed away."

Revelation 21:1-4

82 Farther Along

Rev. W. B. Stevens | Rev. W. B. Stevens

1. Tempt-ed and tried, we're oft made to won - der why it should
2. "Faith - ful till death," said our lov - ing Mas - ter, "a few more
3. When we see Je - sus com-ing in glo - ry, when He comes
be thus, all the day long. While there are oth - ers liv - ing a -
days to la - bor and wait." Toils of the road will then seem as
from His home in the sky. Then we shall meet Him in that bright
REFRAIN
bout us, nev - er mo - lest - ed tho' in the wrong.
noth - ing as we sweep through the beau - ti - ful gate. Far-ther a -
man - sion; We'll un - der - stand it all by and by.
long we'll know all a - bout it; Far-ther a - long we'll un-der-stand why. Cheer up, my

E♭ E♭7 Fm/A♭ A♭ Fm/A♭ E♭ A♭/E♭ E♭ Cm7 Fm Fm2 B♭7 E♭
broth - er, live in the sun - shine; We'll un - der - stand it all by and by.

Surely the Presence of the Lord Is in This Place

83

Lanny Wolfe | Lanny Wolfe

D F♯m7 GM9 Em7 D/E
Sure - ly the pres - ence of the Lord is in this place; I can
Em7 F♯m/A A7 G/A A7 D G/A F♯m/A A7
feel His might - y pow - er and His grace. I can
D F♯m7 GM9 G Em7
hear the brush of an - gels' wings, I see glo - ry on each face;
Em7 F♯m/A A7 F♯m/A Em7 F♯m/A A7 D
Sure - ly the pres - ence of the Lord is in this place.

84 I'm Standing on the Solid Rock

Harold Lane

Harold Lane

1. Through my dis - ap-point-ments, strife and dis - con - tent-ment, I
2. E - ven though He's gone now, I don't feel a - lone now, With
3. Now I'm press-ing on-ward, Each step leads me home-ward, I'm
cast my ev - ery care on the Lord. No mat - ter what ob - ses - sion,
com-fort came the Spir - it of the Lord. Now with His Word to guide me,
trust-ing in my Sav-ior day by day; And close is our re - la - tion,
pain or deep de-pres - sion, I'm stand-ing on the Sol - id Rock.
from temp-ta-tions hide me, I'm stand-ing on the Sol - id Rock.
firm is its foun-da - tion, So on this Sol - id Rock I'll stay.
REFRAIN
I'm stand - ing on the Rock of A - ges,
Stand-ing on the Rock, on the Rock of A - ges.

C7 B♭6/D C7/E B♭6/D C7 F Gm/F F
Safe from all the storm that ra - ges;
Safe from ev - ery storm, all the storm that ra - ges.
F Dm FM7/C Dm F F/A F/C C♯°7 Dm
Rich, but not from Sa - tan's wa - ges. I'm
Rich in love, I'm rich, not from Sa tan's wa – ges.
F Dm B♭m6/D♭ F/C C7 F B♭/F F
stand - ing on the Sol - id Rock.

Now in Christ Jesus you who once were far away have been brought near through the blood of Christ.

For he himself is our peace…He came and preached peace to you who were far away and peace to those who were near. For through him we both have access to the Father by one Spirit.

Consequently, you are no longer foreigners and aliens, but fellow citizens with God's people and members of God's household, built on the foundation of the apostles and prophets, with Christ Jesus himself as the chief cornerstone. In him the whole building is joined together and rises to become a holy temple in the Lord. And in him you too are being built together to become a dwelling in which God lives by his Spirit.

Ephesians 2:13-14a, 17-22

85 What a Savior

Marvin P. Dalton Marvin P. Dalton

1. Once I was stray - ing in sin's dark val - ley; No hope with-
2. He left the Fa - ther wtih all His rich - es; With calm - ness
3. Death's chill-y wa - ters I'll soon be cross - ing; His hand will
in could I see. They searched thro' heav - en and found a
sweet and se - rene. Came down from heav - en and gave His
lead me safe o'er. I'll join the cho - sen in that great
Sav - ior To save a poor lost soul like me.
life - blood To make the vil - est sin - ner clean.
cit - y, And sing up there for - ev - er more.
REFRAIN
O what a Sav - ior, O hal - le - lu - jah! His heart was
bro - ken on Cal - va - ry. His hands were nail - scarred,

D♭ C/D♭ D♭7 E♭m/G♭ G♭ A♭/G♭ G♭ D♭ G♭/D♭ Fm/A♭ A♭7 D♭
His side was riv - en. He gave His life - blood for e - ven me.

Surrendered, Completely Surrendered 86

Stephen R. Adams

Stephen R. Adams

C F/C C Dm/C C CM7/E E♭°7 Dm7 G7
Sur - ren - dered, com - plete - ly sur - ren - dered;
G7 Dm7 C/D F/G G7 C G7
What - ev - er He wants, I'll o - bey.
G7 C E+ E7 G/F F C6/E Dm7
Sur - ren - dered, com - plete - ly sur - ren - dered;
F C/G F6 C/E Dm7 Em/G G7 C
His will is my peace for to - day.

87 Jesus Is Coming Soon

R. E. Winsett R. E. Winsett

E♭ B♭ E♭ Cm G
1. Trou - ble - some times are here, fill - ing men's hearts with
2. Love of so man - y cold, los - ing their home of
3. Trou - bles will soon be o'er, hap - py for - ev - er -
Cm E♭ B♭ E♭ E♭/G B♭/F E♭ B♭ F B♭
fear, Free - dom we all hold dear now is at stake;
gold, This in God's Word is told, e - vils a - bound;
more, When we meet on that shore, free from all care;
N.C. E♭ B♭ E♭ Cm G
Hum - bling your heart to God, saves from the chast - 'ning
When these signs come to pass, near - ing the end at
Ris - ing up in the sky, tell - ing this world good -
Cm E♭ B♭7 E♭ B♭7 E♭/B♭ B♭7 E♭ A♭/E♭ E♭
rod, Seek the way pil - grims trod, Chris - tians, a - wake.
last, It will come ver - y fast, trum - pets will sound.
by, Home - ward we then will fly, glo - ry to share.

REFRAIN
N.C. E♭ A♭ E♭ E♭ B♭ E♭
Je-sus is com - ing soon, morn-ing or night or noon, Man-y will
com - ing soon, night or noon,
Cm G Cm B♭ F
meet their doom, trum-pets will sound.
Man - y will meet their doom, trum-pets will sure - ly
B♭ E♭ A♭ E♭ E♭ B♭ E♭
All of the dead shall rise, righ - teous meet in the skies,
sound. dead shall rise, in the skies,
E♭ Cm G Cm Cm7 B♭7 Gm/B♭ B♭7 E♭ A♭/E♭ E♭
Go - ing where no one dies– heav - en bound.
Go-ing where no one dies–

88 While Ages Roll

Mosie Lister Mosie Lister

1. Some - day this stam-m'ring tongue will fal - ter no more, And a grand - er, sweet - er song I shall sing; For I'll join the ran-somed choir on Heav-en's bright shore, For - ev - er to praise the King.
2. When a mil - lion years have passed in that won-der - ful place, My song of praise will just have be - gun; For my joy will nev - er end while I look on His face, And my song will nev - er be done.
REFRAIN
And while the a - ges roll, I'll keep on prais - ing Him, And my voice will nev - er tire or grow old;

A♭ A♭sus A♭ A♭° A♭ D♭/A♭ A♭7 Fm/A♭ A♭7 D♭ D♭sus D♭
And my song shall ev - er be, “Praise the Lamb, who died for
A♭ D♭/A♭ Cm/E♭ E♭7 Cm/E♭ E♭9 Cm/E♭ E♭7 A♭
me!” And I’ll sing it while a - ges shall roll.

After this I looked and there before me was a great multitude that no one could count, from every nation, tribe, people and language, standing before the throne and in front of the Lamb. They were wearing white robes and were holding palm branches in their hands. And they cried out in a loud voice:

> “Salvation belongs to our God,
> who sits on the throne, and to the Lamb.”

All the angels were standing around the throne and around the elders and the four living creatures. They fell down on their faces before the throne and worshiped God, saying:

> “Amen!
> Praise and glory and wisdom and thanks and honor
> and power and strength be to our God for ever and ever.
> Amen!”

These in white robes…these are they who…have washed their robes and made them white in the blood of the Lamb. Therefore, they are before the throne of God and serve him day and night in his temple; and he who sits on the throne will spread his tent over them. Never again will they hunger; never again will they thirst…For the Lamb at the center of the throne will be their shepherd; he will lead them to springs of living water. And God will wipe away every tear from their eyes.

Revelation 14:9-17

89 The Unclouded Day

J. K. Alwood J. K. Alwood

1. O they tell me of a home far be - yond the skies; O they
2. O they tell me of a home where my friends have gone; O they
3. O they tell me of a King in His beau - ty there, And they
4. O they tell me that He smiles on His chil - dren there, And His
tell me of a home far a - way. O they tell me of a home where no
tell me of that land far a - way Where the Tree of Life in e -
tell me that mine eyes shall be - hold Where He sits on the throne that is
smile drives their sor-rows all a - way; And they tell me that no tears ev - er
storm - clouds rise; O they tell me of an un - cloud-ed day.
ter - nal bloom Sheds its fra-grance thro' the un - cloud-ed day.
whit - er than snow, In that ci - ty that is made of gold.
come a - gain In that love - ly land of un - cloud-ed day.
REFRAIN
O the land of cloud-less day! O the land of an un-cloud-ed sky! O they

tell me of a home where no storm-clouds rise; O they tell me of an un-cloud-ed day.

Where the Spirit of the Lord Is

90

Stephen R. Adams

Stephen R. Adams

Where the Spir - it of the Lord is, there is peace; Where the
Spir - it of the Lord is, there is love. There is com-fort in life's
dark - est hour, There is light and life, there is help and
pow - er in the Spir - it, in the Spir - it of the Lord.

91 I'm Bound for the Kingdom

Mosie Lister

Mosie Lister

1. You may ask me where I'm head - ed; you may ask me where I'm bound. Well, I'm go - ing to a coun-try 'cross the sea; And I know I'll have a man - sion, and I know I'll have a crown, Well, I'm bound for the King-dom of the free.
2. Well, I'm go - ing to a coun - try where they say we'll nev - er die. 'Twill be end - less joy and glo - ry there for me; Yes, I know I'll love for - ev - er in that cit - y in the sky, Well, I'm bound for the King-dom of the free.

REFRAIN
C+ F F7/A
Yes, I'm bound for the King-dom of the
Gm/B♭ B♭ F B♭/F F Dm7/A F/A
bless-ed and the free, And my Je-sus soon is
G7 Em/G G7 F/C C/E Dm C7 F/A C9/G F B♭/F F
com-ing af-ter me. There is noth-ing to com-
me, af-ter me.
F FM7 F7 F7/A Gm/B♭ B♭ F C+
pare with the glo-ry o-ver there. Yes, I'm
F F° F G7 C7 F B♭ F
bound for the King-dom of the free.

92 WHAT A DAY!

A Hymn Sequence

We Shall See Jesus
What a Day That Will Be

93 We Shall See Jesus

Diane Wilkinson

Diane Wilkinson
Arranged by Marty Parks

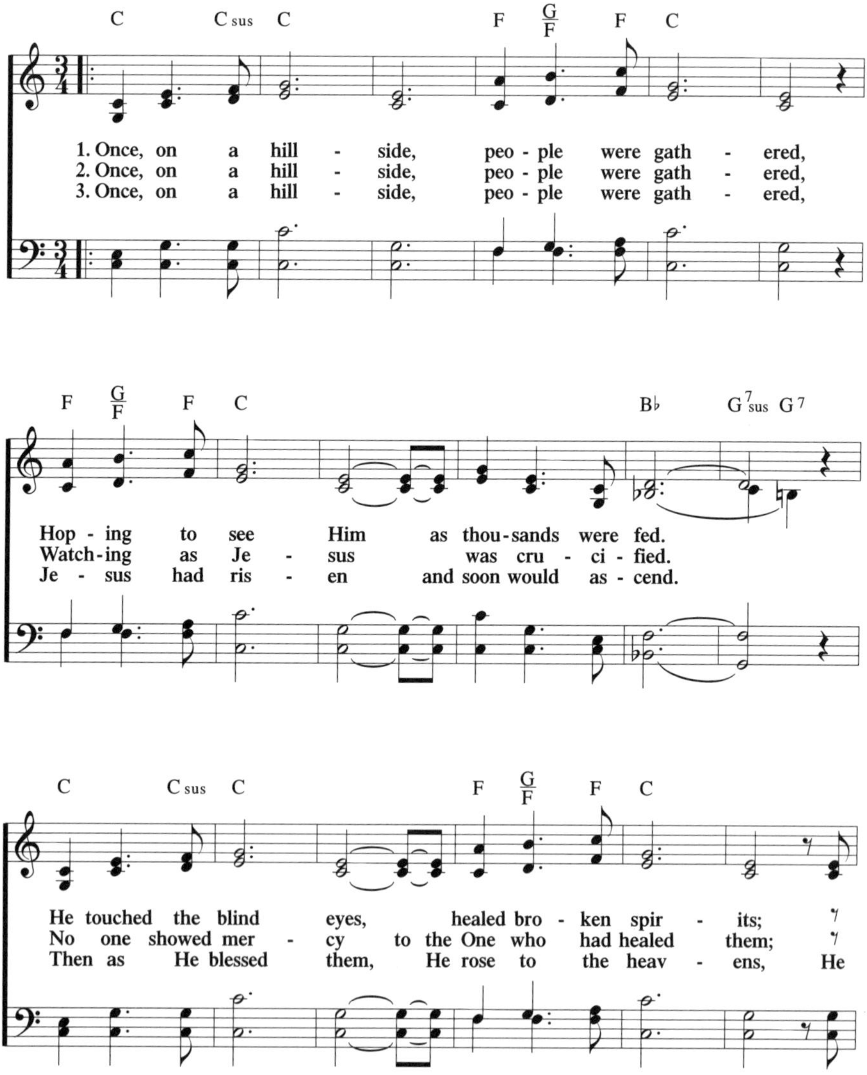
C Csus C F G/F F C
1. Once, on a hill - side, peo - ple were gath - ered,
2. Once, on a hill - side, peo - ple were gath - ered,
3. Once, on a hill - side, peo - ple were gath - ered,
F G/F F C B♭ G7sus G7
Hop - ing to see Him as thou - sands were fed.
Watch - ing as Je - sus was cru - ci - fied.
Je - sus had ris - en and soon would as - cend.
C Csus C F G/F F C
He touched the blind eyes, healed bro - ken spir - its;
No one showed mer - cy to the One who had healed them;
Then as He blessed them, He rose to the heav - ens, He

F G/F F C Am7 Dm Em/G G7
1, 2
Csus C
Moved with com - pas - sion, He raised up the dead.
Yet Je - sus loved them as He suf - fered and died.
gave them His prom - ise to come back a -
3
Csus C
REFRAIN
G F/G G7/D C C7 C9 F
gain.
We shall see Je - sus just as they saw Him,
F G/F F C/G Am Am7 D9 D7 Dm Dm7 G7
There is no great - er prom - ise than this.
G F/G G7/D C C7 C9 F
When He re - turns in pow - er and glo - ry,
F G/F F C/G Am G7 Em/G G7 Csus C
We shall see Je - sus just as He is.

Optional transition to "What a Day That Will Be"

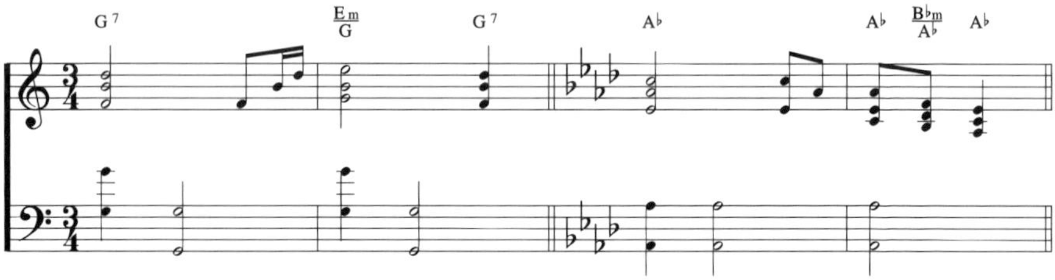

94 What a Day That Will Be

Jim Hill | Jim Hill

1. There is com - ing a day when no heart - aches shall come–
2. There'll be no sor - row there, no more bur - dens to bear,
No more clouds in the sky, no more tears to dim the eye. All is
No more sick - ness, no pain, no more part - ing o - ver there. And for-
peace for - ev - er - more on that hap - py gold-en shore. What a day,
ev - er I will be with the One who died for me. What a day,
glo - ri - ous day that will be!
glo - ri - ous day that will be!
REFRAIN
What a day that will be when my

Je - sus I shall see, And I look up-on His face– the One who
saved me by His grace. When He takes me by the hand and leads me
thro' the Prom-ised Land, What a day, glo-ri-ous day that will be!

End of Hymn Sequence "WHAT A DAY!"

How great is the love the Father has lavished on us, that we should be called children of God! And that is what we are! The reason the world does not know us is that it did not know him.

Dear friends, now we are children of God, and what we will be has not yet been made known. But we know that when he appears, we shall be like him, for we shall see him as he is.

1 John 3: 1-2

95 Blessed Assurance

Fanny J. Crosby

Phoebe Palmer Knapp

1. Bless-ed as - sur - ance, Je - sus is mine! O what a fore - taste of
2. Per - fect sub - mis - sion, per-fect de - light! Vi - sions of rap - ture now
3. Per - fect sub - mis - sion, all is at rest. I in my Sav - ior am
glo - ry di - vine! Heir of sal - va - tion, pur-chase of God, Born of His
burst on my sight! An - gels de - scend - ing bring from a - bove Ech - oes of
hap - py and blest– Watch-ing and wait - ing, look - ing a - bove, Filled with His
Spir - it, washed in His blood!
mer - cy, whis-pers of love.
good - ness, lost in His love.
REFRAIN
This is my sto - ry, this is my song, Prais-ing my Sav - ior all the day long.
This is my sto - ry, this is my song, Prais-ing my Sav - ior all the day long.

Where Could I Go? 96

James B. Coats James B. Coats

F F7 F7/A B♭ F
1. Liv - ing be - low in this old sin - ful world
2. Neigh - bors are kind, I love them ev - ery one–
3. Life here is grand with friends I love so dear,
REFRAIN Where could I go? O where could I go
F Fsus F C7/E F Csus C
Hard - ly a com - fort can af - ford;
We get a - long in sweet ac - cord;
Com - fort I get from God's own Word;
Seek - ing a ref - uge for my soul?
F F7 F7/A B♭ F
Striv - ing a - lone to face temp - ta - tion sore,
But when my soul needs man - na from a - bove,
Yet when I face the chill - ing hand of death,
Need - ing a friend to save me in the end,
F F7/A Gm/B♭ F/C Dm C7 F B♭/F F
Where could I go but to the Lord?
Where could I go but to the Lord?

97 He Will Pilot Me

Charles T. Bailey
Byron L. Whitworth

A♭ D♭/A♭ A♭ A♭/C B♭ B♭9
1. Al - though I can - not see the way, O'er life's tem - pes - tuous
2. Dark clouds may gath - er in the sky, And rough the sea may
3. Dear Lord, what - e'er the storm may be, I'll sim - ply trust in
E♭ B♭7/F E♭ A♭
sea; (dark sea;) I know that Je - sus is my Friend, And
be; (may be;) His love shall ev - er be my song, I
Thee; (in Thee;) Re - ly - ing on Thy love so true, To
A♭ B♭m/D♭ A♭/E♭ E♭7 A♭ D♭/A♭ A♭
REFRAIN
that He'll pi - lot me.
know He'll pi - lot me.
safe - ly pi - lot me.
pi - lot me.
He'll pi - lot
By His hand He'll
A♭ D♭ A♭
me from day to day, When
pi - lot me, O - ver life's tem - pes - tuous sea,

E♭7 Fm B♭7
blind - ed eyes can't see the
When my blind - ed eyes can't see, Can - not see the
E♭/G B♭7/F E♭ A♭
way; Let come what may on
way, the way; Come what may, let come what may,
D♭ A♭ F7
life's dark sea, My bless - ed
On life's dark and storm - y sea; My dear Lord,
B♭7 A♭/E♭ E♭7 A♭ A♭° A♭
Lord will pi - lot me.
bless - ed Lord. He will pi - lot, pi - lot me.

[Jesus] got up, rebuked the wind and said to the waves, "Quiet! Be still!" Then the wind died down and it was completely calm.

He said to his disciples, "Why are you so afraid? Do you still have no faith?"

They were terrified and asked each other, "Who is this? Even the wind and the waves obey him!"

Mark 4:39-41

98 He Hideth My Soul

Fanny J. Crosby

William J. Kirkpatrick

1. A wonderful Savior is Jesus my Lord, A wonderful Savior to me; He hideth my soul in the cleft of the rock, Where rivers of pleasure I see.
2. A wonderful Savior is Jesus my Lord– He taketh my burden away. He holdeth me up, and I shall not be moved; He giveth me strength as my day.
3. With numberless blessings each moment He crowns; And, filled with His fullness divine, I sing in my rapture, "O glory to God For such a Redeemer as mine!"
4. When clothed in His brightness, transported I rise To meet Him in clouds of the sky; His perfect salvation, His wonderful love I'll shout with the millions on high!
REFRAIN
He hideth my soul in the cleft of the rock That shadows a dry, thirsty land; He hideth my life in the depths of His love And

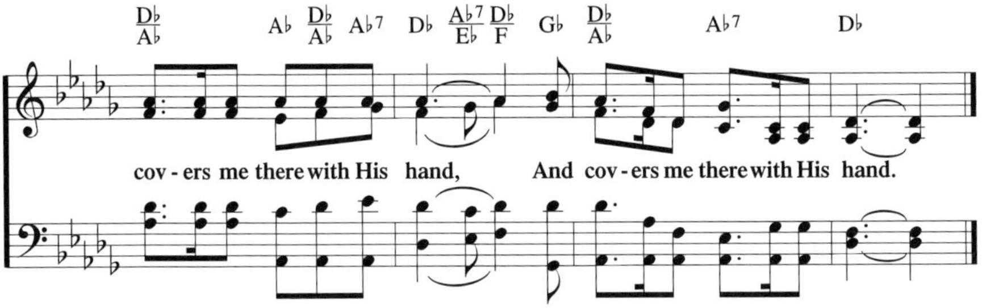
cov - ers me there with His hand, And cov - ers me there with His hand.

Peace in the Midst of the Storm 99

Stephen R. Adams Stephen R. Adams

There is peace in the midst of the storm - tossed life;
O there's an An-chor, there's a Rock to cast my faith up - on.
Je - sus rides in my ves - sel so I'll fear no a - larm;
He gives me peace in the midst of my storm.

100 Restore My Soul

Mosie Lister

Mosie Lister

C Csus C Dm/C C G7
1. Lord, You know that I've been fool - ish, I've been blind;
2. Stripped of all that once I clung to, Lord, I come;
G7 C/G Dm/G C/G G7 C/G Dm/G C
I've let my doubts and my con - fu - sions cloud my mind.
Tho' in Your eyes I know I'm noth - ing, yet I come.
C Dm/C C7 F/C C7 Dm/C C C9 C7 F
I have walked in my own wis - dom; I've been wrong.
With Your hand that once was nail - scarred just for me,
Am7 D D7 G/D D7 G
Take my hand and lead me back where I be - long.
Touch me now and make me all that I should be.

REFRAIN
Re - store my soul in the val - ley, That I might be
wor - thy at last To stand with Thee on the top of the
moun - tain, In the val - ley, re - store my soul.

Have mercy on me, O God, according to your unfailing love;
    according to your great compassion blot out my transgressions.
Wash away all my iniquity and cleanse me from my sin.
    For I know my transgressions, and my sin is always before me.
Cleanse me with hyssop, and I will be clean;
    wash me, and I will be whiter than snow.
Create in me a clean heart, O God, and renew a steadfast spirit within me.
Do not cast me from your presence or take your Holy Spirit from me.
    Restore to me the joy of your salvation.

Psalm 51:1-3, 7, 10-12

101 I Know Who Holds Tomorrow

Ira Stanphill Ira Stanphill

B♭ Cm/B♭ B♭ B♭° B♭ Gm/B♭ B♭ B♭9/D B♭/D E♭
1. I don't know a-bout to-mor-row, I just live
2. Ev-ery step is get-ting bright-er as the gold-
3. I don't know a-bout to-mor-row, It may bring
E♭ F/E♭ E♭ B♭ B♭7/D E♭ F/E♭ E♭
from day to day; I don't bor-row from its
en stairs I climb; Ev-ery bur-den's get-ting
me pov-er-ty; But the one who feeds the
B♭ G7 G+ G7 C7 C9 Am/C C7 F7
sun-shine, For its skies may turn to gray;
light-er, Ev-ery cloud is sil-ver lined;
spar-row, Is the one who stands by me;
F7 E♭/G F/A B♭ B♭° B♭ Gm/B♭ B♭ B♭9/D B♭7/D
I don't wor-ry o'er the fu-ture, For I
There the sun is al-ways shin-ing, There no
And the path that be my por-tion, May be

E♭ F/E♭ E♭ B♭ B♭7/D E♭
know what Je - sus said, And to - day
tear will dim the eye; At the end -
thro' the flame or flood; But His pres -
E♭ F/E♭ E♭ B♭ E♭/G E♭m/G♭ B♭/F F9 Dm/F F7
I'll walk be - side Him, For He knows what is a -
ing of the rain-bow, Where the moun - tains touch the
ence goes be - fore me, And I'm cov - ered with His
REFRAIN
B♭ B♭7 E♭ E♭° E♭ E♭/B♭ B♭
head.
sky. Man - y things a - bout to - mor - row I don't
blood.
C7 C9 Am/C C7 F7sus F7 B♭ Cm/B♭ B♭ B♭9 B♭7
seem to un - der - stand; But I know who holds to -
E♭ E♭/G E♭m/G♭ B♭/F F7 B♭
mor - row, And I know who holds my hand.

102 He Knows Just What I Need

Mosie Lister

Mosie Lister

1. My Je - sus knows when I am lone - ly, He knows each pain, He sees each tear. He un - der - stands each lone - ly heart - ache; He un - der - stands and al - ways cares.
2. My Je - sus knows when I am bur - dened; He knows how much my heart can bear. He lifts me up when I am sink - ing, And bring me joy be - yond com - pare.
3. When oth - er friends seem to for - sake me, When skies are dark, when hope seems gone; By faith I feel His arms a - bout me, And hear Him say, "You're not a - lone."
REFRAIN
My Je - sus know just what I need. Oh yes, He knows just what I need. He sat - is -

fies, and ev-ery need sup-plies, Yes, He knows just what I need.

O Say But I'm Glad

James P. Sullivan

Mildred Sullivan Lacour

1. There is a song in my heart to-day, Some-thing I nev - er had.
2. Won - der-ful, mar-vel - ous love He brings In - to a heart that's sad.
3. Won't you come to Him with all your care, Wea - ry and worn and sad?
Je - sus has tak - en my sin a - way. O say, but I'm glad.
Thro' dark - est tun - nels the soul just sings. O say, but I'm glad.
You, too, will sing as His love you share, O say, but I'm glad.
REFRAIN
O say, but I'm glad, I'm glad; O say, but I'm glad!
Je - sus has come and my cup's o-ver-run, O say, but I'm glad.

104 Dwelling in Beulah Land

C. Austin Miles | C. Austin Miles

B♭ B♭sus B♭ E♭/B♭ B♭ E♭/B♭ B♭ B♭/F Gm/F F F7 B♭
1. Far a - bove the noise of strife up - on my ear is fall - ing,
2. Far be - low the storm of doubt up - on the world is beat - ing,
3. Let the storm - y breez - es blow, their cry can - not a - larm me;
4. View - ing here the works of God, I sink in con - tem - pla - tion,
E♭ F/E♭ E♭ B♭ C7 C C9 F7
Then I know the sins of earth be - set on ev - ery hand.
sons of men in bat - tle long the en - e - my with - stand;
I am safe - ly shel - tered here, pro - tect - ed by God's hand;
Hear - ing now His bless - ed voice, I see the way He planned;
B♭ B♭sus B♭ E♭/B♭ B♭ E♭/B♭ B♭ B♭/F Gm/F F F7 B♭
Doubt and fear and things of earth in vain to me are call - ing,
Safe am I with - in the cas - tle of God's Word re - treat - ing,
Here the sun is al - ways shin - ing, here there's naught can harm me,
Dwell - ing in the Spir - it here I learn of full sal - va - tion,
E♭ F/E♭ E♭ B♭/F E♭ B♭/F F7 B♭
None of these shall move me from Beu - lah land.
Noth - ing then can reach me– 'tis Beu - lah land.
I am safe for - ev - er in Beu - lah land.
Glad - ly will I tar - ry in Beu - lah land.

REFRAIN
I'm liv - ing on the moun-tain, un - der-neath a cloud - less
sky, I'm drink-ing at the foun-tain that nev - er shall run
Praise God!
dry; O yes, I'm feast - ing on the man - na from a boun - ti - ful sup -
ply, For I am dwell-ing in Beu - lah land.

You will be called by a new name
that the mouth of the Lord will bestow.
You will be a crown of splendor in the Lord's hand,
a royal diadem in the hand of your God.
No longer will they call you Deserted,
or name your land Desolate.
But you will be called Hephzibah, and your land Beulah;
for the Lord will take delight in you.

Isaiah 62:2-4

105 GOD'S AMAZING GRACE

A Hymn Sequence

Amazing Grace
Grace Greater Than Our Sin
All Because of God's Amazing Grace

106 Amazing Grace

John Newton;
stanza 5, anonymous

Virginia Harmony, 1831

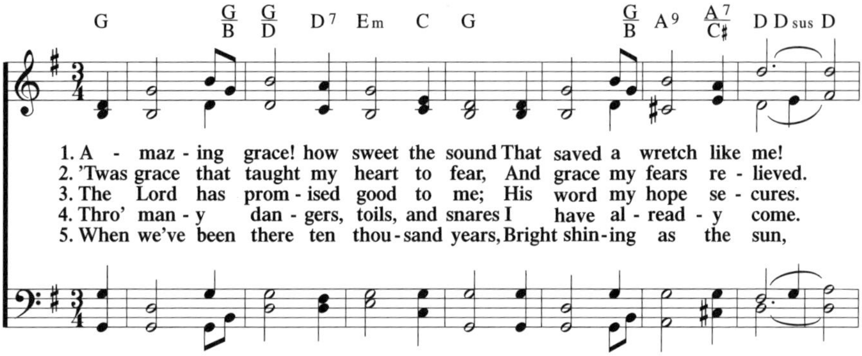
G G/B G/D D7 Em C G G/B A9 A7/C♯ D Dsus D
1. A - maz - ing grace! how sweet the sound That saved a wretch like me!
2. 'Twas grace that taught my heart to fear, And grace my fears re - lieved.
3. The Lord has prom - ised good to me; His word my hope se - cures.
4. Thro' man - y dan - gers, toils, and snares I have al - read - y come.
5. When we've been there ten thou - sand years, Bright shin - ing as the sun,

G G/B C/G G/B C G Bm Em G/D D7 G
I once was lost, but now am found; Was blind, but now I see.
How pre - cious did that grace ap - pear The hour I first be - lieved!
He will my shield and por - tion be As long as life en - dures.
'Tis grace hath bro't me safe thus far, And grace will lead me home.
We've no less days to sing God's praise Than when we'd first be - gun.

Optional transition to "Grace Greater than Our Sin"

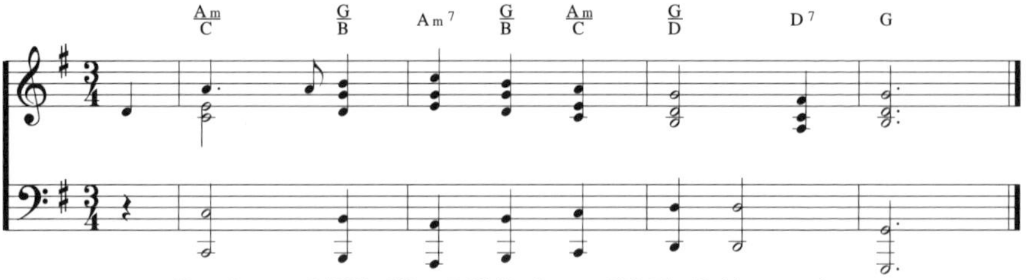
Am/C G/B Am7 G/B Am/C G/D D7 G

Grace Greater than Our Sin

Julia H. Johnston

Daniel B. Towner

1. Mar - vel - ous grace of our lov - ing Lord, Grace that ex - ceeds our sin and our guilt, Yon - der on Cal - va - ry's mount out - poured, There where the blood of the Lamb was spilt!
2. Sin and de - spair, like the sea waves cold, Threat - en the soul with in - fi - nite loss. Grace that is great - er, yes, grace un - told, Points to the ref - uge, the might - y cross.
3. Dark is the stain that we can - not hide, What can a - vail to wash it a - way? Look! there is flow - ing a crim - son tide; Whit - er than snow you may be to - day.
4. Mar - vel - ous, in - fi - nite, match - less grace, Free - ly be - stowed on all who be - lieve! You that are long - ing to see His face, Will you this mo-ment His grace re - ceive?
REFRAIN
Grace, grace, God's grace,
Mar - vel - ous grace, in - fi - nite grace,
Grace that will par - don and cleanse with - in!
Grace, grace, God's grace,
Mar - vel - ous grace, in - fi - nite grace,
Grace that is great - er than all our sin!

Optional transition to "All Because of God's Amazing Grace"

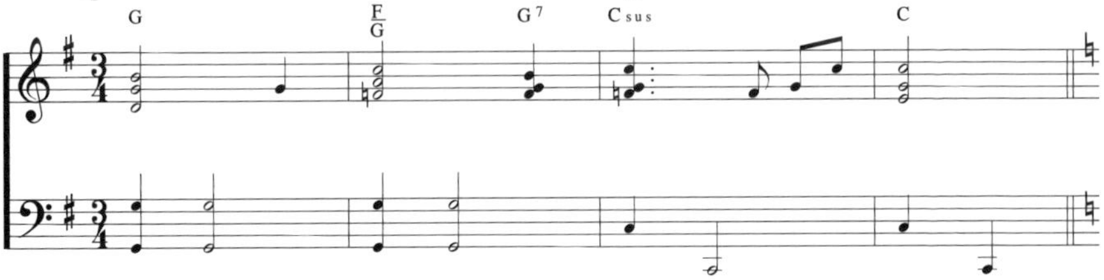

108 All Because of God's Amazing Grace

Stephen R. Adams — Stephen R. Adams

1. A - maz - ing grace– O how sweet the sound That
2. Thro' dis - ap - point - ment and dan - ger, too, Thro'
saved a poor sin - ner like me! Tho' once I was lost, yet
la - bors and sor - rows we've come! But God's grace has guid - ed
now I'm found; Tho' I was blind-ed, now I see!
safe - ly thro', And it will sure - ly lead us home!
REFRAIN
And it's all be - cause of God's a - maz - ing grace!

G/B Am Am7 D7 Dm7/G G7
Be - cause on Cal-v'ry's moun-tain He took my place!
G C B♭/C C7 F G/F
And some-day, some glo-rious morn - ing, I shall see Him face to
F G/F F C F/A F C/G G7 C
face, All be - cause of God's a - maz - ing grace!

End of Hymn Sequence "GOD'S AMAZING GRACE"

Because of his great love for us, God, who is rich in mercy, made us alive with Christ even when we were dead in transgressions–it is by grace you have been saved. And God raised us up with Christ and seated us with him in the heavenly realms in Christ Jesus, in order that in the coming ages he might show the incomparable riches of his grace, expressed in his kindness to us in Christ Jesus.

For it is by grace you have been saved, through faith–and this not from yourselves, it is the gift of God.

Ephesians 2:4-8

109 We Are So Blessed

William J. and Gloria Gaither

William J. Gaither and Greg Nelson
Arranged by Keith Phillips

We are so blessed by the gifts from Your hand, I just
so blessed, we just can't find a way Or the
can't un - der - stand why You've loved us so much. We are
words that can say thank You,
Lord, for Your touch. When we're emp - ty You fill us 'til
we o - ver - flow. When we're hun - gry You feed us and cause us to
know. We are so blessed, take what we have to

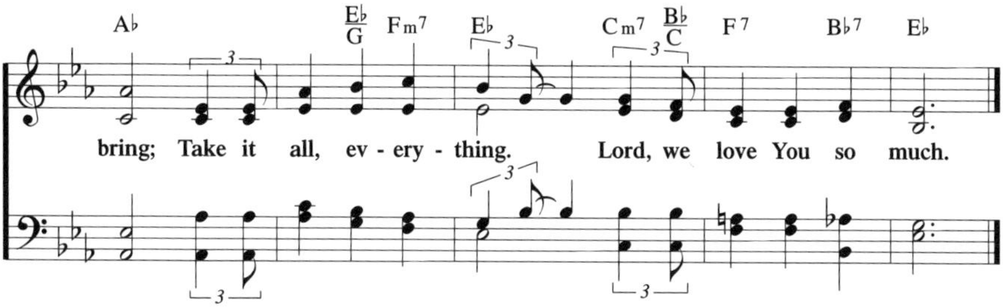
A♭ E♭/G Fm7 E♭ Cm7 B♭/C F7 B♭7 E♭
bring; Take it all, ev - ery - thing. Lord, we love You so much.

One of Your Children Needs You, Lord 110

Mosie Lister

Mosie Lister

B♭ B♭sus B♭ E♭
1. One of Your chil - dren needs You, Lord.
2. One of Your chil - dren is cry - ing, Lord.
3. One of Your chil - dren loves You, Lord.
C7 Dm/C C7 F F7
One of Your chil - dren needs You, Lord.
One of Your chil - dren is cry - ing, Lord.
One of Your chil - dren loves You, Lord.
B♭ E♭/B♭ B♭7/D Fm/E♭ E♭
One of Your chil - dren needs You, Lord.
One of Your chil - dren is cry - ing, Lord.
One of Your chil - dren loves You, Lord.
B♭/F F Dm/F F7 B♭
Je - sus, Je - sus, be near.
Je - sus, Je - sus, be near.
Je - sus, Je - sus, be near.

111 I Saw the Light

Hank Williams

Hank Williams
Arranged by Marty Parks

F Dm/F F/C F Dm/F F
1. I wan-dered so aim - less, my life filled with sin,
2. Just like a blind man I wan-dered a - long,
B♭ Gm/B♭ B♭ F
I would - n't let my dear Sav - ior in;
Wor-ries and fears I claimed for my own;
F Dm/F F/C F Gm/C F
Then Je - sus came like a strang - er in the night,
Then like a blind man that God gave back his sight,
F B♭/F F Am/C C7 F
Praise the Lord, I saw the light.
Praise the Lord, I saw the light.
REFRAIN
F F° F/C Gm/F F/C F F° F/C Gm/F F/A Gm/B♭ B♭
I saw the light, I saw the light; No more
light, yes,

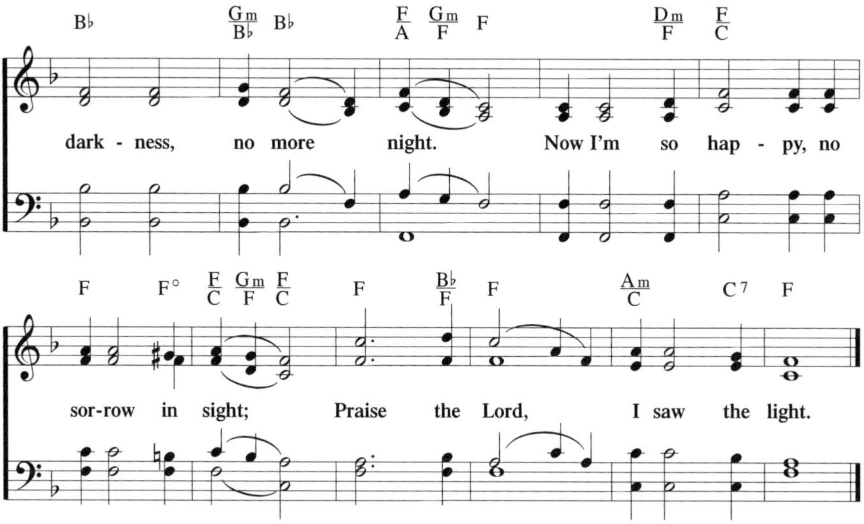
B♭ Gm/B♭ B♭ F/A Gm/F F Dm/F F/C
dark - ness, no more night. Now I'm so hap - py, no
F F° F/C Gm/F F/C F B♭/F F Am/C C7 F
sor-row in sight; Praise the Lord, I saw the light.

Saul was still breathing out murderous threats against the Lord's disciples. He went to the high priest and asked him for letters to the synagogues in Damascus, so that if he found any there who belonged to the Way, whether men or women, he might take them as prisoners to Jerusalem.

As he neared Damascus on his journey, suddenly a light from heaven flashed around him. He fell to the ground and heard a voice say to him, "Saul, Saul, why do you persecute me?"

"Who are you, Lord?" Saul asked.

"I am Jesus, whom you are persecuting," he replied. "Now get up and go into the city, and you will be told what you must do."

Acts 9:1-6

112 Wonderful

Haldor Lillenas — Haldor Lillenas

1. O my heart sings to - day, sings for joy and glad - ness, Je - sus saves,
2. Once a slave, now I'm free, free from con-dem-na - tion. Je - sus gives
3. Liv - ing here with my Lord in a ho - ly un - ion, Day by day,
sat - is - fies, takes a - way my sad - ness. Guilt is gone; peace is mine,
lib - er - ty and a full sal - va - tion. Now the sins of the past
all the way, hold-ing sweet com-mun - ion. O what change grace hath wrought
peace like to a riv - er. Je - sus is won-der-ful, might-y to de - liv - er.
have been all for-giv - en, And my name is in-scribed in the book of heav - en.
in my low-ly sta - tion Since my soul has re-ceived full and free sal - va - tion!
REFRAIN
Won-der - ful, won-der - ful, Je - sus is to me! Coun - sel - or,

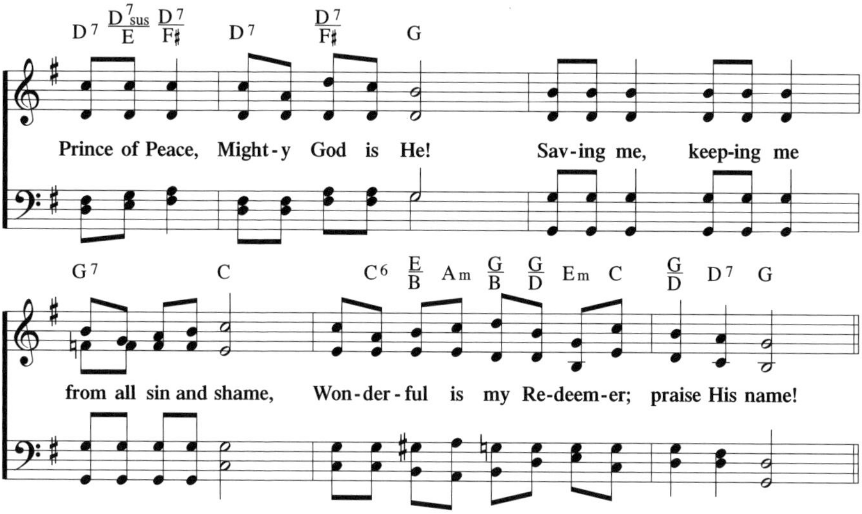
D7 D7sus/E D7/F♯ D7 D7/F♯ G
Prince of Peace, Might-y God is He! Sav-ing me, keep-ing me
G7 C C6 E/B Am G/B G/D Em C G/D D7 G
from all sin and shame, Won-der-ful is my Re-deem-er; praise His name!

Come, Holy Spirit

113

Gloria Gaither and William J. Gaither

William J. Gaither

F B♭/F F F/C Csus C7 Gm
Come, Ho-ly Spir-it, I need You; Come, sweet
B♭/C Am/C C7 F2 F F7 E♭/F F7
Spir-it, I pray. Come in Your strength and Your
Cm/B♭ B♭ Gm F/C C7 F
pow-er; Come in Your own gen-tle way.

114 Touring That City

Harold Lane

Harold Lane

E♭ Fm/E♭ E♭ E♭°7 E♭ A♭/E♭ E♭
1. Man - y times I have won-dered 'bout the sights of that
2. Here on earth we have trou-bles that to us seem so
E♭ E♭7 E♭9 A♭ A♭sus A♭ E♭
cit - y And all that my eyes shall be - hold.
heav-y, But in heav - en no one will be sad.
E♭ Fm/E♭ E♭ E♭° E♭ A♭/E♭ E♭
I will see all the won-ders when I en - ter that
Mom and Dad will be sing - ing, heav-en's praise will be
E♭ E♭/B♭ D°7/B Cm B♭7 Gm/B♭ B♭7 E♭
cit - y, There for - ev - er to be safe in His fold.
ring - ing For the dear - est Friend I ev - er had.
REFRAIN
E♭ E♭7 E♭9
Some morn - ing you'll find me tour - ing that cit - y Where the

A♭ B♭/A♭ A♭ E♭
Son of God is the Light. You'll find me there on the
E♭ F7/C F7 B♭7
streets so pret-ty, Made of gold so pure and so bright.
B♭7 E♭ E♭7 E♭9
With Je-sus, the One who gave me the vic-t'ry, Who
A♭ B♭/A♭ A♭ E♭
led me a-cross the di-vide. Some morn-ing you'll find me
E♭ E♭/B♭ D°7/B Cm B♭7 Gm/B♭ B♭7 E♭
tour-ing that cit-y Where with Him I will ev-er a-bide.

115 Heaven's Jubilee

Adger M. Pace

G. T. Speer

1. Some glad morn-ing we shall see Je-sus in the air, Com-ing af-ter
2. Seems that now I al-most see all the saint-ed dead, Ris-ing for that
3. When with all that heav'n-ly host we be-gin to sing, Sing-ing in the
you and me, joy is ours to share; What re-joic-ing there will be
ju-bi-lee that is just a-head; In the twink-ling of an eye,
Ho-ly Ghost, how the heav'ns will ring; Mil-lions there will join the song,
when the saints shall rise, Head-ed for that ju-bi-lee, yon-der in the skies.
changed with them to be, All the liv-ing saints to fly to that ju-bi-lee.
with them we shall be, Prais-ing Christ thro' a-ges long, heav-en's ju-bi-lee.
REFRAIN
Oh, what sing-ing, Oh, what shout-ing,
What a day of sing-ing, sing-ing, What a day of shout-ing, shout-ing,

A♭ E♭7 Fm B♭7 E♭ B♭/F E♭7
On that hap - py morn - ing when we all shall rise;
On that hap - py morn - ing when we all shall glad - ly rise;
A♭
Oh, what glo - ry, Hal - le - lu - jah!
What a day of glo ry, glo - ry, Glo - ry hal - le - lu - jah! Glo - ry!
A♭ E♭7 Fm A♭/E♭ E♭7 A♭ D♭7/A♭ A♭
When we meet our bless - ed Sav - ior in the skies.
When we meet our bless - ed Sav - ior yon - der in the skies.

"Do not let your hearts be troubled.
    Trust in God; trust also in me.
In my Father's house are many rooms;
    if it were not so, I would have told you.
I am going there to prepare a place for you.
    And if I go and prepare a place for you,
I will come back and take you to be with me
    that you also may be where I am."

John 14:1-3

116 Little Is Much When God Is in It

Kittie L. Suffield — Kittie L. Suffield

1. In the har - vest field now rip-ened There's a work for all to do.
2. Does the place you're called to la - bor Seem so small and lit - tle known?
3. Are you laid a - side from ser-vice, Bod - y worn from toil and care?
4. When the con - flict here is end-ed And our race on earth is run,
Hark! the voice of God is call-ing To the har - vest call-ing you.
It is great if God is in it, And He'll not for - get His own.
You can still be in the bat-tle In the sa - cred place of prayer.
He will say, if we are faith-ful, "Wel-come home, My child, well done!"
REFRAIN
Lit-tle is much when God is in it! La - bor not for wealth or fame.
There's a crown– and you can win it, If you go in Je - sus' name.

Let Me Touch Him

Vep Ellis

Vep Ellis

1. Let me touch Him, let me touch Je-sus, Let me touch Him as He pass-es by; Then when I shall reach out to oth-ers, They shall know Him, they shall live and not die.
2. I was stray-ing so far from Je-sus, I was lone-ly, had no peace with-in; Then the hand of my Savior touched me, Now I'm reach-ing to oth-ers in sin.
3. There's a riv-er, a riv-er flow-ing From with-in and to cleanse my soul; And the flow sets my life to glow-ing, Ho-ly Spir-it, more than sil-ver and gold.
REFRAIN
O to be His hand extend-ed, Reach-ing out to the op-pressed; Let me touch Him, let me touch Je-sus, So that oth-ers may know and be blessed.

118 Come and Dine

C. B. Widmeyer C. B. Widmeyer

Bb Bbsus Bb Eb/Bb Bb Eb Ebsus Eb
1. Je - sus has a ta - ble spread Where the saints of God are fed;
2. The dis - ci - ples came to land, Thus o - bey - ing Christ's com - mand;
3. Soon the Lamb will take His bride To be ev - er at His side;
Cm7 F F7 Eb/F Dm/F F9 Dm/F Bb
He in - vites His cho - sen peo - ple, "Come and dine."
For the Mas - ter called to them, "O come and dine."
All the hosts of heav - en will as - sem - bled be.
Bb Bbsus Bb Eb/Bb Bb Eb Ebsus Eb
With His man - na He doth feed And sup - plies our ev - ery need.
There they found their heart's de - sire– Bread and fish up - on the fire;
O 'twill be a glo-rious sight– All the saints in spot - less white;
Cm7 F7 Eb/F F7 F9 F7 Bb
O 'tis sweet to sup with Je - sus all the time!
Thus He sat - is - fies the hun - gry ev - ery time.
And with Je - sus they will feast e - ter - nal - ly.
REFRAIN
Bb F7 F9 Bb F7/C Bb/D Bb
"Come and dine," the Mas - ter call - eth, "come and dine." You may
dine, come and dine."

E♭ G7/D C7 Am/C C7 F C7/E F B♭ Dm/F F7 B♭
feast at Je-sus' ta-ble all the time. He who fed the mul-ti-tude,
time, all the time.
B♭ D+ D7 E♭ F7 E♭/F F7 B♭
turned the wa-ter in-to wine, To the hun-gry call-eth now, "Come and dine."

Early in the morning, Jesus stood on the shore, but the disciples did not realize that it was Jesus.

He called out to them, "Friends, haven't you any fish?"

"No," they answered.

He said, "Throw your net on the right side of the boat and you will find some." When they did, they were unable to haul the net in because of the large number of fish.

Then the disciple whom Jesus loved said to Peter, "It is the Lord!"

When they landed, they saw a fire of burning coals there with fish on it, and some bread…

Jesus said to them, "Come and have breakfast."

John 21:4-7a, 9, 12

119 There Is Joy in My Soul

Fanny Crosby

Paul Ferrin

1. I will not be wea-ry, tho' tri-als may come, And trou-bles be-fore me I see; But count them as noth-ing com-pared with the love Of Je-sus, my Sav-ior, to me.
2. I can-not be wea-ry when He is my Rest, What-e'er my temp-ta-tions may be, I'll trust in His prom-ise be-cause He has said: "My grace is suf-fi-cient for thee."
3. There's joy that no lan-guage or thought can ex-press; It comes from His pres-ence di-vine. And when in His like-ness at last I a-wake, Its full-ness, I know, will be mine!
REFRAIN
I'll sing of His love, of His won-der-ful love, Tho' won-der-ful moun-tains may roll. I fear not the tem-pest, I

dread not the storm, For Je - sus gives joy to my soul

'Tis So Sweet to Trust in Jesus 120

Louisa M. R. Stead | William J. Kirkpatrick

1. 'Tis so sweet to trust in Je - sus, Just to take Him at His Word,
2. O how sweet to trust in Je - sus, Just to trust His cleans-ing blood,
3. Yes, 'tis sweet to trust in Je - sus, Just from sin and self to cease,
4. I'm so glad I learned to trust Thee, Pre - cious Je - sus, Sav - ior, Friend;
Just to rest up - on His prom - ise, Just to know: "Thus saith the Lord."
Just in sim - ple faith to plunge me 'Neath the heal - ing, cleans-ing flood!
Just from Je - sus sim - ply tak - ing Life and rest, and joy and peace.
And I know that Thou art with me, Wilt be with me to the end.
REFRAIN
Je - sus, Je - sus, how I trust Him! How I've proved Him o'er and o'er!
Je - sus, Je - sus, pre - cious Je - sus! O for grace to trust Him more!

121

The King and I

Mosie Lister

Mosie Lister

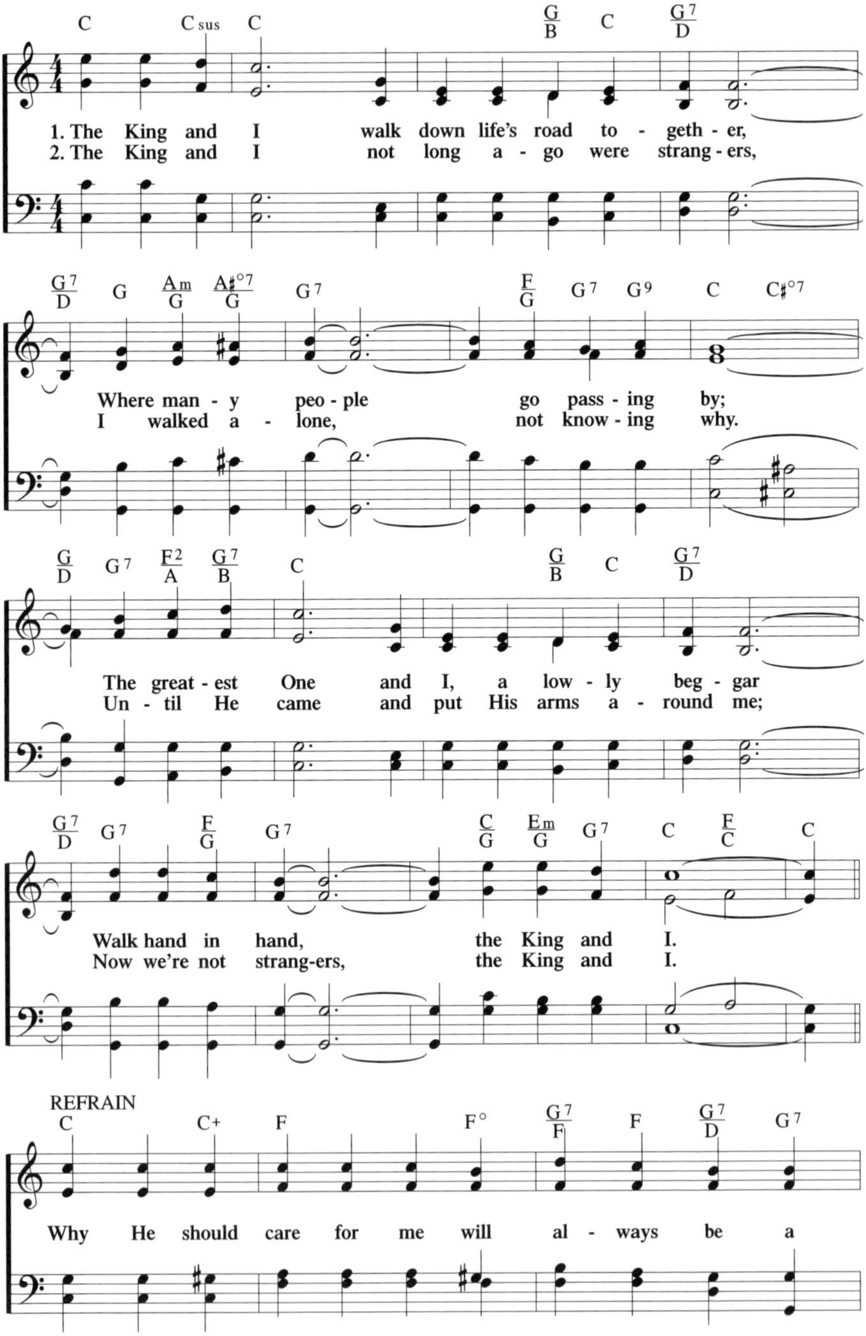
C Csus C G/B C G7/D
1. The King and I walk down life's road to - geth - er,
2. The King and I not long a - go were strang - ers,
G7/D G Am/G A♯°7/G G7 F/G G7 G9 C C♯°7
Where man - y peo - ple go pass - ing by;
I walked a - lone, not know - ing why.
G/D G7 F2/A G7/B C G/B C G7/D
The great - est One and I, a low - ly beg - gar
Un - til He came and put His arms a - round me;
G7/D G7 F/G G7 C/G Em/G G7 C F/C C
Walk hand in hand, the King and I.
Now we're not strang-ers, the King and I.
REFRAIN
C C+ F F° G7/F F G7/D G7
Why He should care for me will al - ways be a

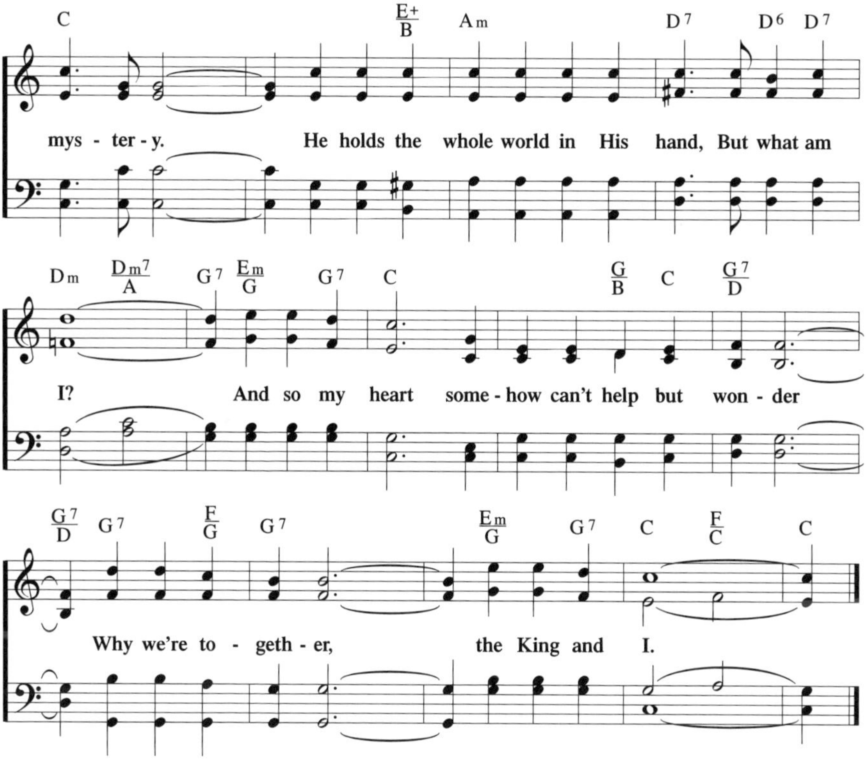
C E+/B Am D7 D6 D7
mys - ter - y. He holds the whole world in His hand, But what am
Dm Dm7/A G7 Em/G G7 C G/B C G7/D
I? And so my heart some - how can't help but won - der
G7/D G7 F/G G7 Em/G G7 C F/C C
Why we're to - geth - er, the King and I.

I am always with you;
you hold me by my right hand.
You guide me with your counsel,
and afterward you will take me into glory.
Whom have I in heaven but you?
And earth has nothing I desire besides you.
My flesh and my heart may fail,
but God is the strength of my heart
and my portion forever.
Those who are far from you will perish;
you destroy all who are unfaithful to you.
But as for me, it is good to be near God.
I have made the Sovereign Lord my refuge.
I will tell of all your deeds.

Psalm 73:23-28

122 Child of the King

Cindy Walker | Cindy Walker

1. Once I was clothed in the rags of my sin, Wretch-ed and
2. Now I'm a child with a Heav - en - ly home, My Ho - ly
poor, lost and lone - ly with - in; But with won - d'rous com - pas - sion the
Fa - ther had made me His own; And I'm cleansed by His blood and I'm
King of all kings, In pit - y and love, took me un - der His wing.
clothed in His love, And some - day I'll sing with the an - gels a - bove.
REFRAIN
O yes, O yes, I'm a child of the King. His roy - al
blood now flows in my veins; And I, who was wretch-ed and

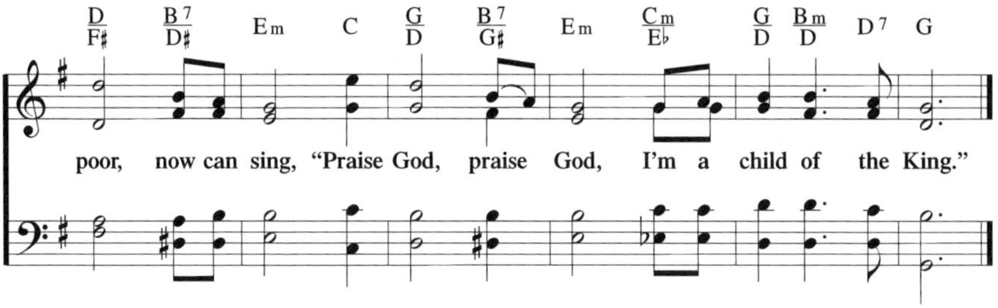
D/F♯ B7/D♯ Em C G/D B7/G♯ Em Cm/E♭ G/D Bm/D D7 G
poor, now can sing, "Praise God, praise God, I'm a child of the King."

One Flock, One Shepherd

123

Stephen R. Adams Stephen R. Adams

B♭/C C7 F E♭/F B♭ B♭/F F B♭/F B♭m6/F F D7
We are one flock, one Shep-herd; The sweet-est sto - ry

D7 G7 C7 B♭/C C7 F E♭/F F7 E♭/F B♭
that has ev - er been told. We are one flock led by one

B♭m6 F Cm6/E♭ D+ D7 G7 B♭6/C F B♭/F F
Shep - herd; And some-day He will bring us to one fold.

124 God Said It...I Believe It...That Settles It

Stephen R. Adams
and Gene Braun

Stephen R. Adams
Arranged by Marty Parks

God said it, and I be-lieve it, and that set-tles it for me!
God said it, and I be-lieve it, and that set-tles it for me!
Tho' some may doubt that His Word is true, I've cho-sen to be-lieve it, now
how a-bout you? God said it, and I be-lieve it, and that set-tles it for me!

125 PRAISE THE LAMB

A Hymn Sequence

I Will Praise Him
Behold the Lamb

I Will Praise Him

Margaret J. Harris — Margaret J. Harris

1. When I saw the cleans - ing foun - tain, O - pen wide for all my sin,
2. Tho' the way seems straight and nar - row, All I claimed was swept a - way;
3. Then God's fire up - on the al - tar Of my heart was set a - flame.
4. Bless - ed be the name of Je - sus! I'm so glad He took me in;
5. Glo - ry, glo - ry to the Fa - ther! Glo - ry, glo - ry to the Son!
I o - beyed the Spir - it's woo - ing When He said, "Wilt thou be clean?"
My am - bi - tions, plans and wish - es At my feet in ash - es lay.
I shall nev - er cease to praise Him, Glo - ry, glo - ry to His name!
He's for - giv - en my trans - gres - sions, He has cleansed my heart from sin.
Glo - ry, glo - ry to the Spir - it! Glo - ry to the Three in One!
REFRAIN
I will praise Him! I will praise Him! Praise the Lamb for sin-ners slain;
slain, for sin - ners slain!
Give Him glo-ry, all ye peo - ple, For His blood can wash a - way each stain.
Optional transition to "Behold the Lamb"

127 Behold the Lamb

Dottie Rambo

Dottie Rambo
Arranged by Marty Parks

Be - hold the Lamb, be - hold the Lamb,
Slain from the foun - da - tion of the world.
For sin - ners cru - ci - fied, O ho - ly sac - ri - fice;
Be - hold the Lamb of God, be - hold the Lamb.
Fine
Crown Him, Crown Him; Wor - thy

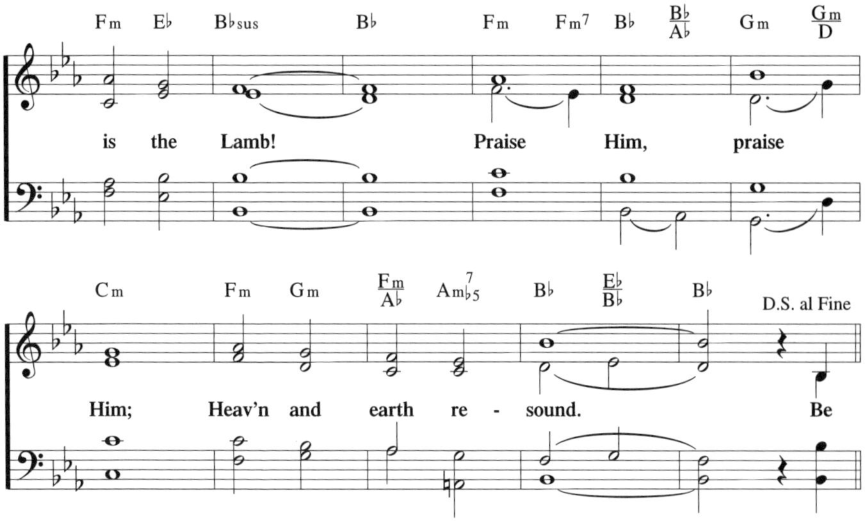

End of Hymn Sequence "PRAISE THE LAMB"

Then I looked and heard the voice of many angels, numbering thousands upon thousands, and ten thousand times ten thousand. They encircled the throne and the living creatures and the elders. In a loud voice they sang:

> "Worthy is the Lamb who was slain,
> to receive power and wealth
> and wisdom and strength
> and honor and glory and praise!"

Then I heard every creature in heaven and on earth and under the earth and on the sea, and all that is in them, singing:

> "To him who sits on the throne and to the Lamb
> be praise and honor and glory and power
> for ever and ever!"

The four living creatures said, "Amen," and the elders fell down and worshiped.

Revelation 5:11-14

128 He Became Poor

Byron Carmony

Byron Carmony

1. They bor-rowed a man-ger of hay for His bed— Je - sus, my Sav - ior. No soft, down - y pil - low, no warm cra - dle spread For Je - sus, my Lord.
2. They bor-rowed a colt, low - ly beast for a King, Je - sus, my Sav - ior. No court gave Him hon - or, no car - il - lons ring For Je - sus, my Lord.
3. He bor-rowed a room for the Pass - o - ver feast, Je - sus, my Sav - ior; Be - com - ing both Ser - vant and Heav - en - ly Priest, This Je - sus, my Lord.
4. They bor-rowed a tomb for the Cru - ci - fied One, Je - sus, my Sav - ior; No mon - u - ment roy - al for God's on - ly Son, For Je - sus, my Lord.
REFRAIN
His were the plan - ets and stars in the sky; His were the val - leys and moun-tains so high. His, all earth's rich - es from pole un - to pole, But He be-came poor to ran - som my soul.

Jesus, the Son of God

Ken Bible and G. T. Haywood

G. T. Haywood

A♭ A♭/C D♭ D♭/A♭ A♭
1. A Child is cry-ing, so help-less and low-ly– Je-sus, the
2. The Light in our dark-ness, the touch of our Fa-ther– Je-sus, the
A♭ A♭/C E♭7 E♭/D♭ C Fsus Fm A♭/E♭ D♭ D♭/F D♭/A♭ A♭
Son of God; Our Lord, our Cre-a-tor, Al-might-y and ho-ly–
Son of God; Our Friend and our Shep-herd, our Hope and our Broth-er–
Fm F♭7 A♭/E♭ E♭7 A♭
Je-sus, the Son of God.
Je-sus, the Son of God.
REFRAIN
O Sweet Won-der!
D♭/A♭ A♭ A♭/C E♭7 C Fsus Fm
O Sweet Won-der! Je-sus, the Son of God. How I a-dore You,
D♭ D♭/F D♭/A♭ A♭ Fm F♭7 A♭/E♭ E♭7 A♭
O how I love You– Je-sus, the Son of God.

130 Sweet, Sweet Spirit

Doris Akers Doris Akers

G Am/G G C G/B Em D G Dm6/F E7 E7♭9/G♯
1. There's a sweet, sweet Spir - it in this place, And I
2. There are bless - ings you can - not re - ceive Till you
Am G/B Am/C G/D Am/D G/D D Em/D D7 G C/G G Am/G
know that it's the Spir - it of the Lord. There are
know Him in His full - ness and be - lieve; You're the
G C G/B Em D G Dm6/F E7 E7♭9/G♯
sweet ex - pres - sions on each face, And I
one to pro - fit when you say, "I am
Am G/B Am/C G/D Am/D G/D D Em/D D7 G C/G G
know they feel the pres - ence of the Lord.
going to walk with Je - sus all the way."

REFRAIN
Sweet Ho - ly Spir - it, sweet heav-en-ly Dove, Stay right here
with us, fill-ing us with Your love. And for these bless-ings we
lift our hearts in praise. With-out a doubt we'll know that we have
been re - vived When we shall leave this place.

Suddenly a sound like the blowing of a violent wind came from heaven and filled the whole house where they were sitting. They saw what seemed to be tongues of fire that separated and came to rest on each of them. All of them were filled with the Holy Spirit.

Acts 2:2-4a

131 I Will Glory in the Cross

Dottie Rambo Dottie Rambo

1. I boast not of works, nor tell of good deeds; For naught have I
2. My tro - phies and crowns, my robe stained with sin, 'Twas all that I
done to mer - it His grace. All glo - ry and praise shall
had to lay at His feet; Un - wor - thy to eat from the
rest up - on Him, So will - ing to die in my place.
ta - ble of life 'Til love made pro - vi - sion for me.
REFRAIN
I will glo - ry in the cross, in the cross, Lest His suf - f'ring
all be in vain. I will weep no more for the

C C6 CM7 Cm6 G/D Bm/D D7 G
cross that He bore; I wll glo - ry in the cross.

I'm So Glad Jesus Lifted Me 132

Traditional and Camp Kirkland

Traditional

A♭ E♭ B♭sus/F E♭/G E♭7
1. I'm so glad Je - sus lift - ed me, I'm so glad,
2. I was lost in sin, Je - sus res-cued me, I was lost in sin,
3. Now I'm heav - en - bound, Je - sus set me free, Now I'm heav - en - bound,
A♭ E♭7 A♭ A♭7 B♭m/D♭ D♭
Je - sus lift - ed me; I'm so glad, Je - sus lift - ed me
Je - sus res - cued me; I was lost in sin, Je - sus res - cued me,
Je - sus set me free; Now I'm heav - en-bound, Je - sus set me free,
D°7 A♭/E♭ C7 Fm B♭9 E♭7 A♭
Sing - ing, "Glo - ry, hal - le - lu - jah!" Je - sus lift - ed me.
Sing - ing, "Glo - ry, hal - le - lu - jah!" Je - sus lift - ed me.
Sing - ing, "Glo - ry, hal - le - lu - jah!" Je - sus lift - ed me.

133 Highway to Heaven

Anonymous — Anonymous

It's a high - way to Heav - en, None can walk up there
but the pure in heart; It's a high - way to Heav - en, Walk-ing up the King's high -
way.
1. My way is bright - er, my load is light - er,
2. If you're not walk - ing, start while I'm talk - ing,
Walk-ing up the King's high - way; There's joy in know - ing,
Walk-ing up the King's high - way; There'll be a bless - ing,
with Him I'm go - ing, Walk-ing up the King's high - way.
you'll be con - fess - ing, Walk-ing up the King's high - way.

E♭ A♭
It's a high - way to
It's a high - way, it's a high - way,
E♭ B♭7
Heav - en, None can walk up there
It's a high-way up to Heav-en. None can walk up there,
E♭ Fm/E♭ E♭ A♭
but the pure in heart; It's a high - way to
but the pure in heart. It's a high-way, it's a high-way,
E♭ E♭7/G Fm/A♭ E♭/B♭ B♭7 E♭
Heav - en,
It's a high-way up to Heav-en. Walk-ing up the King's high - way.

A highway will be there; it will be called the Way of Holiness... only the redeemed will walk there, and the ransomed of the Lord will return. They will enter Zion with singing; everlasting joy will crown their heads. Gladness and joy will overtake them, and sorrow and sighing will flee away.

Isaiah 35:8-10

134 I'll Meet You in the Morning

Albert E. Brumley | Albert E. Brumley

E♭ A♭/E♭ E♭ Fm/A♭ A♭ E♭
1. I will meet you in the morn-ing, by the bright riv - er side, When all
2. I will meet you in the morn-ing, in the sweet by and by, And ex -
3. I will meet you in the morn-ing, at the end of the way, On the
E♭ B♭9 Gm/B♭ D/B♭ E♭
sor - row had drift - ed a - way; I'll be stand - ing at the por - tals,
change the old cross for a crown; There will be no dis - ap - point - ments
streets of that cit - y of gold; Where we all can be to - geth - er
E♭ Fm/A♭ A♭ E♭ B♭/F F B♭/F F7 B♭ B♭7
when the gates o - pen wide, At the close of life's long, drear - y day.
and no - bod - y shall die, In that land where the sun go - eth down.
and be hap - py for aye, While the years and the a - ges shall roll.
REFRAIN
B♭7 E♭
I'll meet you in the morn - ing with a
Meet you in the morn - ing, meet you in the morn - ing,
A♭ E♭ A♭/E♭ E♭
"How do you do?" And we'll sit down by the
"How do you do? How do you do?" Sit down by the riv - er,

E♭ Cm F
riv - er and with rap - ture "auld" ac-quaint-ance re -
sit down by the riv - er, Rap - ture our "auld" ac -
B♭ F/C B♭/D E♭
new. You'll know me in the
quaint - ance re - new. Know me in the morn - ing,
E♭ A♭
morn - ing by the smiles that I
know me in the morn - ing, Smiles that I wear,
E♭ A♭/E♭ E♭
wear, When I meet you in the morn - ing
smiles that I wear. Meet you in the morn-ing, meet you in the morn-ing,
E♭ E♭/B♭ B♭7 Gm/B♭ B♭7 E♭ A♭/E♭ E♭
in the cit - y that is built four square.
Cit - y, cit - y built, that cit - y build four square.

135 The Light from Heaven

Mosie Lister | Mosie Lister

F Gm/F F Fsus F Gm/F F Dm/F
1. Je - sus is the Light, the bright and shin-ing Light Of this and of all worlds to
2. Bright-er grows the way, and sweet-er ev - ery day; We sing as the moun-tain we
C7/G C7 F/C C7 Am/C C7 C F F/C C♯7 Dm Dsus Am/C
come; And I'll fol - low the Light, I'll fol - low day and night, And I
climb. And I'll fol - low the Sun un - til the day is done, And the
B♭ Am/C C7 F REFRAIN C7 F
know that He will lead me home.
shad-ows are all far be - hind.
The Light from heav-en is shin-ing down on
C7 F C7
me, I walk with Je-sus; I'm hap - py, glad and free. The Sun is
F C7 F
shin-ing; the bet-ter way I see, The Light from heav-en is shin-ing down on me.

Yes, I Know

Anna W. Waterman

Anna W. Waterman
Arranged by Marty Parks

1. Come, ye sin - ners lost and lone - ly, Je - sus' blood can make you free. For He saved the worst a - mong you When He saved a wretch like me.
2. To the faint He giv-eth pow - er, Thro' the moun - tains makes a way; Find - eth wat - er in the des - ert, Turns the night to gold - en day.
3. In temp - ta - tion He is near thee, Holds the pow'rs of hell at bay; Guides you to the path of safe - ty, Gives you grace for ev - ery day.
REFRAIN
And I know, yes, I know,
Yes, I know, O yes, I know
Je-sus' blood can make the vil - est sin-ner clean.
And I know, yes, I know,
Yes, I know, O yes, I know
Je-sus' blood can make the vil - est sin-ner clean.

137 My Wonderful Lord

Haldor Lillenas

Haldor Lillenas

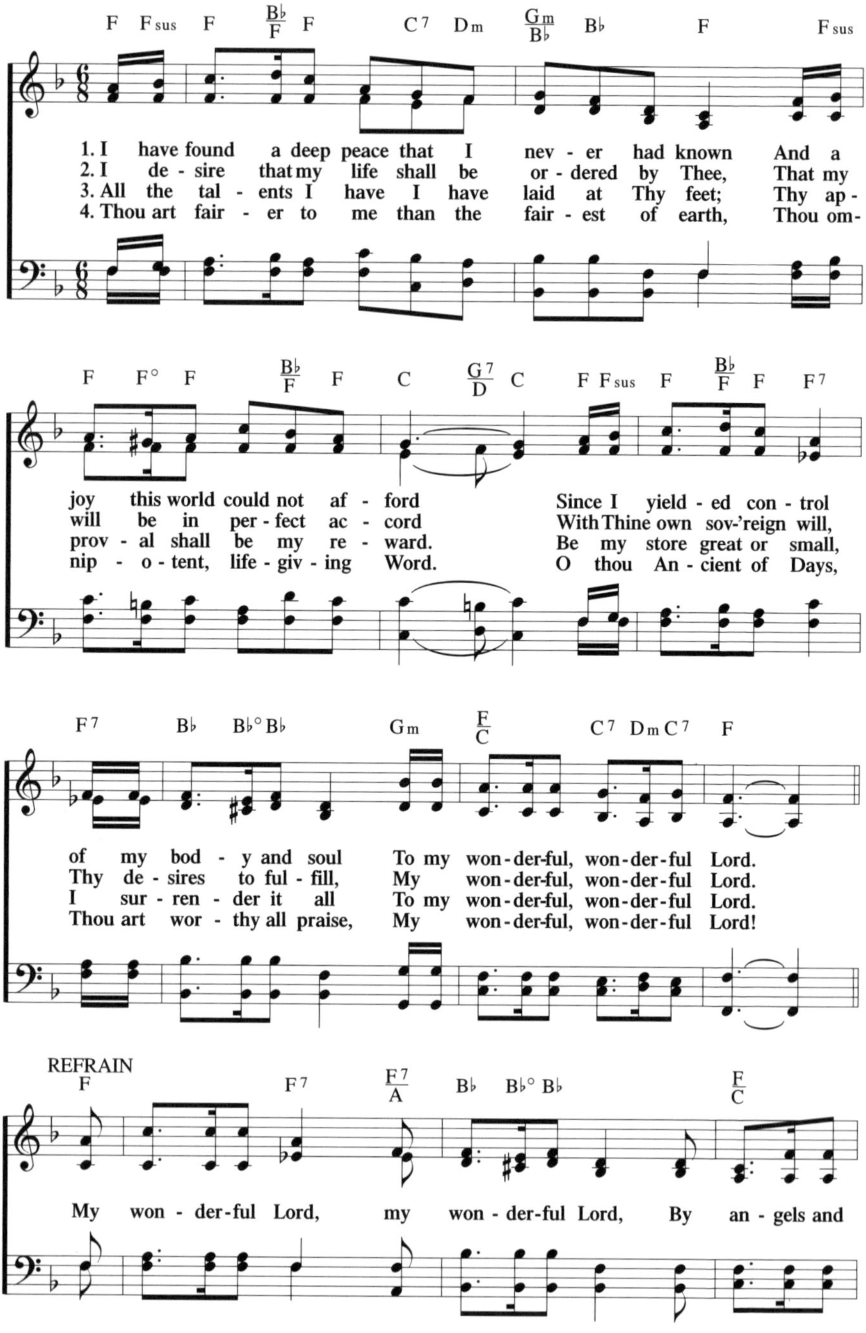
1. I have found a deep peace that I never had known And a joy this world could not afford Since I yield-ed con-trol of my bod-y and soul To my won-der-ful, won-der-ful Lord.
2. I de-sire that my life shall be or-dered by Thee, That my will be in per-fect ac-cord With Thine own sov-'reign will, Thy de-sires to ful-fill, My won-der-ful, won-der-ful Lord.
3. All the tal-ents I have I have laid at Thy feet; Thy ap-prov-al shall be my re-ward. Be my store great or small, I sur-ren-der it all To my won-der-ful, won-der-ful Lord.
4. Thou art fair-er to me than the fair-est of earth, Thou om-nip-o-tent, life-giv-ing Word. O thou An-cient of Days, Thou art wor-thy all praise, My won-der-ful, won-der-ful Lord!
REFRAIN
My won-der-ful Lord, my won-der-ful Lord, By an-gels and

ser - aphs in heav - en a - dored. I bow at Thy shrine, My
Sav - ior di - vine, My won - der-ful, won - der-ful Lord.

He's All I Need

138

Traditional and Ken Bible

Traditional
Arranged by Tom Fettke

1. He's all I need, He's all I need; Je - sus is all I need. He's all I need, He's all I need; Je - sus is all I need.
2. He's good to me, He's good to me; Je - sus is good to me. He's good to me, He's good to me; Je - sus is good to me.
3. He's life and peace, He's life and peace; Je - sus is life and peace. He's life and peace, He's life and peace; Je - sus is life and peace.

139 We'll Soon Be Done with Troubles

Cleavant Derricks — Cleavant Derricks

B♭ E♭/B♭ B♭ E♭/B♭ B♭
1. Some of these days I'm go - ing home where no sor-rows ev - er
2. Kin-dred and friends now wait for me, soon their fac - es I shall
3. I shall be - hold His bless - ed face, I shall feel His match-less
B♭ F/C B♭/D
come.
see. We'll soon be done with trou-bles and
grace.
We'll soon be done,
B♭/F F B♭/D F7/C B♭ Gm/B♭ B♭ B♭9/D
tri - als; Safe from heart-ache, pain and care, we shall
'Tis a home of life so fair and we'll
O what peace and joy sub - lime in that
trou-bles and tri - als;
E♭ N.C. B♭/F D7/F♯ G sus Gm
all that glo - ry share.
all be gath - ered there, Sit down be-side my Je - sus,
home of love di - vine.
And I'm gon - na

N.C.
B♭/F
Dm/F
F7
B♭
REFRAIN
sit down and rest a lit - tle while.
Lord, I'm gon - na
We'll soon be
B♭
Cm/B♭
B♭
E♭/B♭
B♭
We'll soon be done with trou-bles and tri - als.
done,
trou-bles and tri - als, In that
B♭
F7
Dm/F
F7
B♭
N.C.
Yes, in that home on the oth - er side.
home
on the oth - er side. And I'm a gon-na
E♭
B♭
E♭/B♭
B♭
N.C.
Shake glad hands with the eld - ers, tell my kin - dred good morn - ing,
Lord, and
Then I'm gon-na
B♭/F
D7/F♯
G sus
Gm
E♭m6/G♭
B♭/F
Dm/F
F7
B♭
Sit down be - side my Je - sus, gon - na sit down and rest a lit - tle while.
Lord, I'm

140 Peace in the Valley

Thomas A. Dorsey | Thomas A. Dorsey

D♭ E♭m/D♭ D♭ E♭m/D♭ D♭
1. Well, I'm tired and so wea - ry, but I
2. There the flow'rs will be bloom - ing, and the
3. Well, the bear will be gen - tle, and the
G♭ D♭
must go a - long Till the Lord comes and
grass will be green, And the skies will be
wolf will be tame, And the lion shall lay
E♭9 A♭ E♭9/B♭ A♭7 D♭ E♭m/D♭ D♭
calls me a - way, oh yes. Well, the
clear and se - rene, oh yes. Well, the
down by the lamb, oh yes. Well, the
D♭ E♭m/D♭ D♭ G♭
morn - ing is bright and the Lamb is the
sun ev - er beams in this val - ley of
beast from the wild shall be led by a

D♭ E♭7 A♭7
light, And the night, night is fair as the
dreams, And no clouds there will ev - er be
child, And I'll be changed, changed from this crea - ture that I
D♭ E♭m/D♭ D♭ E♭sus/G♭ D♭
REFRAIN
G♭
day, oh yes.
seen, oh yes. There will be peace in the val - ley for
am, oh yes.
D♭ G♭/D♭ D♭ D♭ E♭9
me some - day. There will be peace in the val - ley for
A♭ E♭9/B♭ A♭7 D♭ D♭7
me, oh Lord I pray. There'll be no sad - ness, no sor - row, no
G♭ E♭7 D♭ B♭ B♭7 E♭9 E♭7 A♭7 D♭
trou - ble I see, There will be peace in the val - ley for me.

141 Such Love

C. Bishop

Robert Harkness

1. That God should love a sin - ner such as I, Should yearn to change my
2. That Christ should join so free - ly in the scheme, Al - though it meant His
3. That for a will - ful out - cast such as I The Fa - ther planned, the
4. And now He takes me to His heart– a son; He asks me not to
sor - row in - to bliss, Nor rest till He had planned to bring me nigh–
death on Cal - va - ry– Did ev - er hu - man tongue find no - bler theme
Sav - ior bled and died, Re - demp - tion for a worth - less slave to buy,
fill a ser - vant's place. The far - off coun - try wan - d'rings all are done;
How won - der - ful in love like this!
Than love di - vine that ran - somed me?
Who long had law and grace de - fied!
Wide o - pen are His arms of grace!
REFRAIN
Such love, such won - drous love! Such love, such won - drous love! That
Such love, Such love,
God should love a sin - ner such as I– How won - der - ful is love like this!

Led by the Master's Hand

142

Mosie Lister | Mosie Lister

1. As I walk the road of life, my feet grow wea-ry, And I stum - ble thro' the thorns and shift-ing sand; But I nev - er have a fear a-bout to-mor-row, For I'm led by the Mas - ter's hand.
1. Thro' the val - ley of de-spair tho' I may wan-der, On the high-est moun-tain-top I soon shall stand; And I'll nev - er walk a-lone, for my heart tells me I'll be led by the Mas - ter's hand.
REFRAIN
Thro' the storm, thro' the night I'll keep hold - ing on; With His hand hold-ing mine, hope is nev - er gone. When I climb the last mile to heav-en's land, I'll be led by the Mas - ter's hand.

143 O How I Love Jesus

Frederick Whitfield

Traditional American Melody

1. There is a name I love to hear; I love to sing its worth.
2. It tells me of a Sav - ior's love, Who died to set me free.
3. It tells me what my Fa - ther hath In store for ev - ery day
4. It tells of One whose lov - ing heart Can feel my deep - est woe,
It sounds like mu - sic in my ear, The sweet - est name on earth.
It tells me of His pre - cious blood, The sin - ner's per - fect plea.
And, tho' I tread a dark - some path, Yields sun - shine all the way.
Who in each sor - row bears a part That none can bear be - low.
REFRAIN
O how I love Je - sus! O how I love Je - sus!
O how I love Je - sus, Be - cause He first loved me!

Where No One Stands Alone

Mosie Lister

Mosie Lister

1. Once I stood in the night with my head bowed low, In the
2. Like a king I may live in a pal - ace so tall, With great
dark - ness as black as could be; And my heart felt a - lone and I
rich - es to call my own; But I don't know a thing in this
cried, "O Lord, don't hide Your face from me."
whole wide world that's worse than be - ing a - lone.
REFRAIN
Hold my hand all the
way, Ev - ery hour, ev - ery day, From here to the great un - known.
Take my hand; Let me stand Where no one stands a - lone.

145 Jesus, the Light of the World

George D. Elderkin
and Charles Wesley

George D. Elderkin

1. Hark! the her - ald an - gels sing, Je - sus, the Light of the World;
2. Christ, by high - est heav'n a - dored, Je - sus, the Light of the World;
Glo - ry to the new - born King, Je - sus, the Light of the World.
Christ, the ev - er - last - ing Lord, Je - sus, the Light of the World.
REFRAIN
Walk in the Light, beau - ti - ful Light,
Come where the dew - drops of mer - cy are bright.
Shine all a - round us by

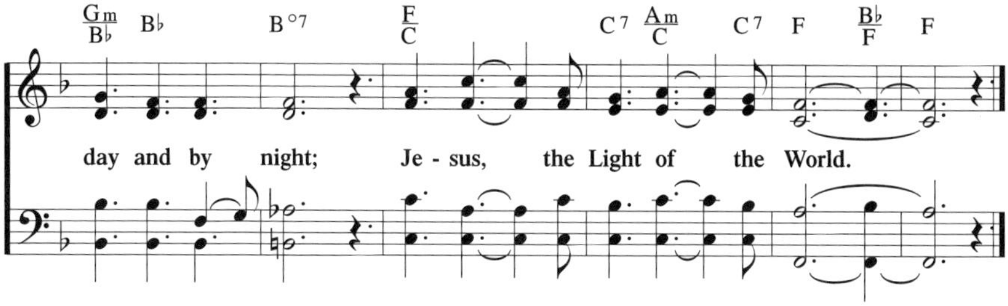
day and by night; Je - sus, the Light of the World.

Sing Praise to the King

146

Mosie Lister

Mosie Lister

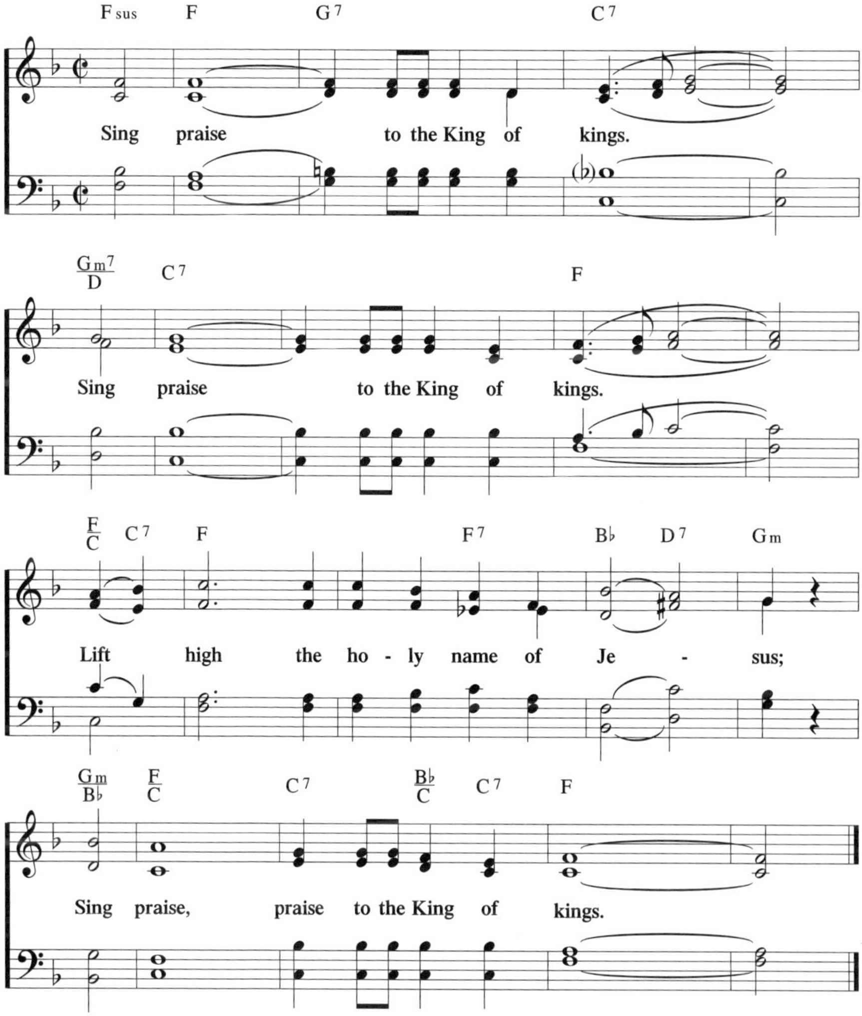
Sing praise to the King of kings.
Sing praise to the King of kings.
Lift high the ho - ly name of Je - sus;
Sing praise, praise to the King of kings.

147 Beautiful Star of Bethlehem

Adger M. Pace R. Fischer Boyce

1. O beau - ti - ful star of Beth - le - hem, shin - ing a -
2. O beau - ti - ful star, the hope of light, guid - ing the
3. O beau - ti - ful star, the hope of rest for the re -
far thro' sha - dows dim, Giv - ing a light for those who
pil - grim thro' the night, O - ver the moun - tain till the
deemed, the good and blessed. Yon - der in glo - ry when the
long have gone. (have gone.) Guid - ing the Wise Men on their
break of dawn, (of dawn,) In - to the light of per - fect
crown is won. (is won.) Je - sus is now that Star di -
way, un - to the place where Je - sus lay. Beau - ti - ful
day it will give out a love - ly ray, Beau - ti - ful
vine, bright - er and bright - er He will shine. Beau - ti - ful

REFRAIN
F Dm7 G7 C13 C7 F B♭/F F B♭/C Gm/C C13
star of Beth - le - hem shine on. (shine on.) O beau - ti - ful
F C F Dm/F F B♭ F Gm/F F
star of Beth - le - hem, Shine up - on
star, O beau - ti - ful star, star of Beth - le - hem.
Am Dm G9 C7 G/D C7 B♭/C Gm/C C13
us un - til the glo - ry dawn; Give us Thy
dawn, the glo - ry dawn;
F Dm/F F C/G F/A B♭ B♭6 B♭ F Gm/F F
light to light the way in - to the land of per - fect day, Beau - ti - ful
F Dm7 G7 C13 C7 F B♭/F FM7 B♭/F F
star of Beth - le - hem shine on.
on, shine on.

148 Room at the Cross for You

Ira F. Stanphill | Ira F. Stanphill

1. The Cross up-on which Je - sus died Is a shel - ter in
2. Tho' mil - lions have found Him a Friend And have turned from the
3. The hand of my Sav - ior is strong, And the love of my
which we can hide, And its grace so free is suf - fi - cient for me,
sins they have sinned. The Sav - ior still waits to o - pen the gates
Sav - ior is long; Thro' sun - shine or rain, thro' loss or in gain,
And deep is its foun - tain– as wide as the sea.
And wel - come a sin - ner be - fore it's too late.
The Blood flows from Cal - v'ry to cleanse ev - ery stain.
REFRAIN
There's room at the Cross for you; There's room at the Cross for you. Tho' mil - lions have come, There's still room for one. Yes, there's room at the Cross for you.

Do You Know My Jesus? 149

Vep Ellis and W. F. Lakey — Vep Ellis and W. F. Lakey

1. Have you a heart that's wea - ry, Tend - ing a load of care?
2. Where is your heart, O pil - grim? What does your light re - veal?
3. Who knows your dis - ap - point - ments? Who hears each time you cry?
Are you a soul that's seek - ing Rest from the bur - den you bear?
Who hears your call for com - fort When naught but sor - row you feel?
Who un - der - stands your heart - aches? Who dries the tears from your eyes?
REFRAIN
Do you know my Je - sus? Do you know my Friend?
Do you know my Je - sus? Do you know my Friend?
Have you heard He loves you, And that He will a - bide till the end?
Have you heard He loves you, end, till the end?

150 It Is No Secret

Stuart Hamblen — Stuart Hamblen

C F G4/F F C F/C C
1. The chimes of time ring out the news; an - oth - er day is through.
2. There is no night, for in His light you'll nev - er walk a - lone;
G7 G°7 G7 C C° C
Some - one slipped and fell. Was that some - one you? You
Al - ways feel at home wher - ev - er you may roam. There
C F G4/F F C F/C C
may have longed for add - ed strength, your cour - age to re - new.
is no pow'r can con - quer you, while God is on your side; Just
G/D Am7 Bm/D D7/F♯ G C/G G7
Do not be dis - heart - ened, for I bring hope to you.
take Him at His prom - ise, don't run a - way and hide.

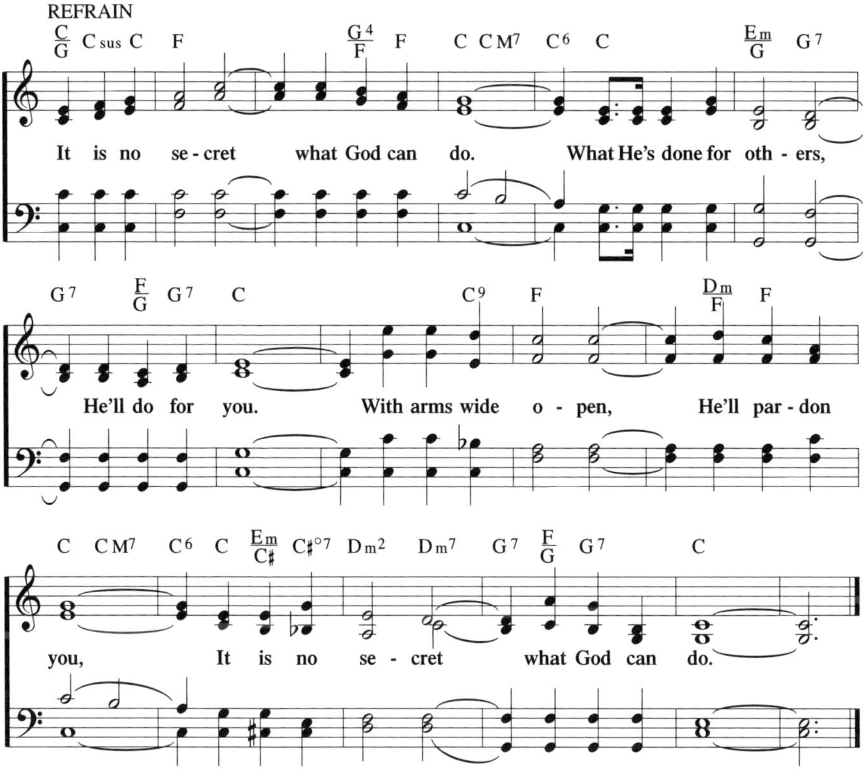
REFRAIN
It is no se - cret what God can do. What He's done for oth - ers,
He'll do for you. With arms wide o - pen, He'll par - don
you, It is no se - cret what God can do.

"There was a man who had two sons. The younger one said to his father, 'Father, give me my share of the estate.' So he divided his property between them.

"Not long after that, the younger son got together all he had, set off for a distant country and there squandered his wealth in wild living.

"When he came to his senses, he said, 'I will set out and go back to my father and say to him: Father I have sinned against heaven and against you. I am no longer worthy to be called your son; make me like one of your hired men.'

"But while he was still a long way off, his father saw him and was filled with compassion for him; he ran to his son, threw his arms around him and kissed him.

"The father said to his servants, 'Quick! Bring the best robe and put it on him. Put a ring on his finger and sandals on his feet. Bring the fattened calf and kill it. Let's have a feast and celebrate. For this son of mine was dead and is alive again; he was lost and is found'"

Luke 15:11-13, 17-19, 20, 22-24

TOPICAL INDEX

Song and *MEDLEY* Titles

HOLY SPIRIT

INVITATION

PRAISE & WORSHIP

PRAYER

REJOICING & TESTIMONY

Alphabetical Index

Song and *MEDLEY* Titles